3D SYNTHETIC ENVIRONMENT RECONSTRUCTION

The Kluwer International Series
in Engineering and Computer Science

3D SYNTHETIC ENVIRONMENT RECONSTRUCTION

Edited by

Mahdi Abdelguerfi
University of New Orleans, U.S.A.

KLUWER ACADEMIC PUBLISHERS
Boston / Dordrecht / London

Distributors for North, Central and South America:
Kluwer Academic Publishers
101 Philip Drive
Assinippi Park
Norwell, Massachusetts 02061 USA
Telephone (781) 871-6600   Fax (781) 681-9045
E-Mail <kluwer@wkap.com>

Distributors for all other countries:
Kluwer Academic Publishers Group
Distribution Centre
Post Office Box 322
3300 AH Dordrecht, THE NETHERLANDS
Telephone 31 78 6392 392   Fax 31 78 6392 254
E-Mail <services@wkap.nl>

   Electronic Services <http://www.wkap.nl>

Library of Congress Cataloging-in-Publication Data

3D synthetic environment reconstruction / edited by Mahdi Abdelguerfi.
   p. cm. – (Kluwer international series in engineering and computer science; SECS 611)
Includes bibliographical references and index.
ISBN 0-7923-7321-9 (alk. paper)
   1. Digital computer simulation. 2. Mathematical models. 3. Computer graphics. I.
Title. II. Series.

QA76.9.C65 A25 2001
006.6'93—dc21   2001016499

Printed on acid-free paper.   Printed in the United States of America

*The Publisher offers discounts on this book for course use and bulk purchases. For
further information, send email to <scott.delman@wkap.com> .*

*The cover art shows a 3D synthetic environment of part of the US Marine Corps'
Military Operations in Urban Terrain facility at Camp LeJeune, NC. This synthetic
environment was generated from a commercial-off-the-shelf database management
system and VPF+. VPF+ adds 3D topology to the National Imagery and Mapping
Agency's Vector Product Format standard and is the result of research by the Naval
Research Laboratory and the University of New Orleans.*

Table of Contents

Preface

A *synthetic environment* can be described as the presentation of one or more aspects of some given real-world environment in a digital simulation, which typically includes visual as well as experiential components. The visual component provides the user with a realistic, three-dimensional, replication of the real world. It includes terrain and terrain features (natural and man made); complex 3D objects; the ocean; the ocean bottom and its associated features; the atmosphere; and near space. In addition, a synthetic environment includes attributes of the objects in the environment, as well as the relationships amongst these objects.

The experiential component immerses the user in the synthetic world by providing a set of interactions with that world consistent with the application area. For example, allowed interactions may allow the user to fly the aircraft using synthetic controls or to explore an urban area to learn the layout of its streets, buildings, etc. In both cases, associated sounds and other environmental conditions can be added for increased realism.

Although synthetic environments were traditionally used in a military setting for mission rehearsal and simulations, their use is rapidly spreading to a variety of applications in the commercial, research and industrial sectors. Included in the many applications for synthetic environments are flight training for commercial aircraft as well as the Space Shuttle, city planning, car safety research in real-time traffic simulations, and video games. The growing popularity of synthetic environments in such areas may be due to the benefits often associated with their use. Automobile manufacturers, for example, can bring a new design to the testing stage in a synthetic environment where necessary modifications can be detected long before the first physical prototype is ever built. City planners are able to visually examine and understand the full impact of new urban development. NASA has found synthetic environments for Space Shuttle mission training more cost effective than physical simulators. In addition, the synthetic environment can be taken aboard the Space Shuttle for continued training during shuttle missions to keep performance at peak. In some cases, projects would be difficult if not impossible without the use of synthetic environments. For example, researchers using synthetic environments have realistically studied motor vehicle/bicycle traffic interactions to better understand ways of decreasing accidents between the two.

This edited manuscript is composed of seven invited chapters from leading experts in the field. The manuscript intends to bring together a coherent body of recent knowledge relating, 3D geospatial data collection, design issues, and techniques used in Synthetic Environments design, implementation and interoperability. In particular, the reader will be exposed to new techniques for the generation, in timely fashion, of Synthetic Environments with increased resolution and rich attribution (this is essential for accurate modeling and simulation). Additionally, interoperability of models and simulations (needed in order to facilitate the reuse of modeling and simulation components) will be dealt with.

The body of coherent work brought by the edited manuscript describes first-hand experiences with Synthetic Environments development. We expect that this proposed manuscript will appeal to a wide audience, ranging from beginners with an interest in Synthetic Environments to experienced practitioners.

The CD-ROM accompanying this manuscript includes a colored version of this manuscript's figures.

Chapter 1

An Overview Of 3D Synthetic Environment Construction

Dr. Roy Ladner, Kevin Shaw
Naval Research Laboratory

Key words: 3D Synthetic Environment, Virtual Reality, 3D-Spatial Database, Vector Product Format

Abstract: This chapter provides introductory material on three-dimensional synthetic environments. Readers are given an understanding of what synthetic environments are and how they are used in varied disciplines along with a look at some of the technologies used for synthetic environment visualization. Readers are provided with an outline of the sources and nature of synthetic environment data and are presented with the challenges associated with constructing realistic synthetic environments.

1. INTRODUCTION

A common conception of *Three-Dimensional Synthetic Environments* (3D SEs) is that of traditional military modeling and simulation (M&S) in which a digital simulation of the natural environment is provided for rehearsal of military operations. However, the use of 3D SEs has grown well beyond M&S to many diverse disciplines such as city planning (Koninger 98, Liggett 95, Tempfli 97), surgical training (Ota 98), manufacturing (Schmeider 98) and education (VETL 98). In contrast to M&S applications, for example, 3D SEs of the human body are being used to train surgeons in the intricacies of delicate surgery (Ota 98). In manufacturing, 3D SEs consisting of new prototype automobiles and the natural environment are being used to test new products before actual production (Schmeider 98). Each of these application areas makes use of an authoritative, three-dimensional digital representation of a given environment.

The Department of Defense (DoD) describes 3D SE in terms of the natural environment, including the terrain, oceans, atmosphere and space (DMSMP 95). Terrain representation involves the composition and representation of the surface of the earth and of the natural and man-made features found there. Representation of the oceans includes the data describing the ocean bottom as well as changes in surface (e.g., sea-state) and sub-surface (e.g., pressure and acoustics) conditions. Atmospheric representations cover the zone from the earth's surface to the upper boundary of the troposphere. Some phenomena of interest there include atmospheric conditions such weather. The latter can also involve four-dimensional representations of natural conditions such as spatial location over time. Space representations cover the area beyond the upper boundary of the troposphere. In addition to representation of the physical environment, the 3D SE may also potentially involve the representation of natural or man-made processes at work in the natural environment, such as seasonal variation or the effects of man's interaction with his world.

This conception of a synthetic environment as a three-dimensional digital representation of the natural environment is not inconsistent with many uses in geographic information systems (GIS), city planning, etc. where accurate simulations of the natural environment and man's impact on the environment are essential. Users are provided with a means of examining the spatial relationships of digital objects that closely resemble their real world counterpart. The ability to model natural processes as well as man-made processes in relation to the natural environment can also be vital to understanding nature and man's impact on it.

Synthetic environment databases can also provide some degree of non-visual information about the environment called *topology* (USAS 98b). Topology in this context refers to the explicit representation of the relationships between objects in the environment. This explicit, pre-computed definition of relationships avoids the need to computationally derive relationships at run-time. Topology means that a GIS application, for example, "knows" that a road allows travel in a certain direction. In some databases, the topological structures are lacking (MULT 96). Image generator applications such as flight simulators do not necessarily need topological information. In other databases the topology is limited to the description of two-dimensional spatial relationships (VPF 96).

The remainder of this chapter provides introductory material about 3D synthetic environments. In order to provide a feel for what 3D SEs are and how they are used, Section 2 gives examples of some of the varied applications that make use of them. Following that, Section 3 examines synthetic environment data sources and introduces various spatial databases used in the synthetic environment domain. The process by which this data is transformed into meaningful 3D SE databases is introduced in Section 4. Section 5 discusses 3D SE database repositories, interchange specifications and distributed simulation applications. The chapter concludes with a look at the technologies that are used for 3D SE visualization. These topics should provide good background material for readers who are interested in exploring this subject in greater detail.

2. 3D SYNTHETIC ENVIRONMENT APPLICATIONS

This section introduces examples of some of the different uses of 3D SEs, namely, in the areas of aerospace, city planning, education, manufacturing and M&S.

1. Aerospace

SEs have been used to train astronauts for Space Shuttle and International Space Stations missions. Figure 1 shows an example of a shared virtual environment in which trainees in the U.S. and Europe were able to practice replacing a solar array drive on the Hubble Telescope. The 3D SE consisted of models of the Hubble Telescope and the cargo bay of the space shuttle. Shared SEs are also in development for training astronauts for maintenance operations within the International Space Station. These uses reduce overall costs of training since trainees are not required to relocate to special facilities in distant countries (Loftin 98).

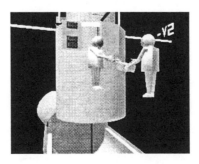

Figure 1. Repairs to the Hubble Telescope are Rehearsed in a Shared SE (Loftin 2000)

2.   City Planning & GIS

The UCLA Urban Simulator shown in Figure 2 is an example of a SE developed for city planning. The Simulator links virtual reality technology with a more traditional Geographic Information System (GIS) database. The system allows planners and designers to evaluate urban development rapidly, in more detail and for less cost than traditional methods (Liggett 95). Similar work on the use of SEs as a tool for city planning is reported in (Koninger 98) and (Tempfli 97).

Figure 2. UCLA Urban Simulator - Detailed Urban Model with Automated Vehicles and Pedestrians (Liggett 95)

3.   Education

Project ScienceSpace is a collection of SEs that enable students to study the dynamics of motion, electrostatics and molecular structures (VETL 98). In one example from that project, shown in Figure 3, objects are given behaviors consistent with their real world counterparts.

Figure 3. An Application Using a SE in Education (VETL 98)

4.   Manufacturing

Daimler-Chrysler has used 3D SEs consisting of driving simulators to test new automobile designs. One of these is shown in Figure 4. The test driver sees the 3D SE consisting of the interior of the vehicle and the roadway in a Head Mounted Display. A correct visual impression of the vehicle is provided to the driver although he may only be sitting in a mock up simulator consisting of a seat, steering wheel, shift lever and pedals. Potential problems can be identified early in the development process long before the physical vehicle is built (Schmeider 98).

Figure 4. Daimler's Driving Simulator (Daimler 99)

5.   M&S

SEs such as that shown in Figure 5 can provide a realistic simulation of a natural environment in which mission rehearsal and training can take place. Among the SE databases created for military M&S are:
- SAKI (Saudi Arabia, Kuwait and Iraq),
- STOW-E (Synthetic Theatre of War - Europe),
- Chorwon (Korea),
- Close Combat Tactical Trainer SE (based on an area in Central Europe but made to resemble the Midwestern U.S.),
- the Mission Training Support System SEs (geospecific SEs constructed from a helicopter pilot's point of view), and
- the Special Operations Forces Aircrew Training System SEs (supporting aircrew training and mission rehearsal) [Trott 96].

The views generated by each of these applications can vary with the needs of the user. An application for a ground vehicle simulation, for example, may provide detailed geometry about the terrain surface and 3D objects on the terrain. Surface slope, soil mobility, the location and the size of obstacles may be provided in sufficient detail in the database so maneuverability could be determined at runtime. A flight simulator, in contrast, may require a texture-mapped image of the terrain instead of data about surface slope (Mamaghani 98). Semi-Automated Forces (SAF) and Computer Generated Forces (CGF) are two applications that make use of topological information (Trott 96). CGF entities are controlled by dynamic, reasoning software models, and 'react' to trainees' actions and the environment without operator input. SAF in contrast accepts some input from a human operator during the interaction with the trainee.

Figure 5. View of a Conceptual M&S SE (ES 99)

3.   SYNTHETIC ENVIRONMENT DATA

1.   Data Sources

NIMA is the primary source of synthetic environment data for the Department of Defense and the private sector. In the 1980's NIMA began the process of transforming their paper mapping data to digital format with a new database specification, Vector Product Format (VPF). Generally, VPF separates data into thematic coverages, with each of these coverages containing thematically consistent data (VPF 96). More details on VPF are given below.

A detailed listing of NIMA's digital data is available in (NIMA). Table 1 lists NIMA's VPF products. Each product is designed to fill different needs. Digital Nautical Chart (DNC) for example, is directed at marine navigation and GIS applications, and it contains significant features collected from harbor, approach, coastal and general charts. Digital Topographic Data

(DTOP) is produced for specific geographic areas and consists of thematic layers from terrain analysis and topographic line maps. Themes include vegetation, transportation, surface materials, surface drainage, obstacles, surface configuration or slope, hydrography, boundaries, population, industry, physiography, utilities and data quality.

Table 1. A Partial Listing of NIMA's VPF Products

Name	Abbreviation
Digital Nautical Chart	DNC
Digital Topographic Data	DTOP
Interim Terrain Data	ITD
Vector Map	VMAP
Urban Vector Map	UVMAP
World Vector Shoreline	WVS
Tactical Terrain Data	TTD
Foundation Feature Data	FFD

Tactical Terrain Data (TTD), consisting of DNC, DTOP and Digital Terrain Elevation Data (described below), is intended to provide data critical to planning and executing joint operations such as close air support missions, amphibious operations and land combat operations. TTD is supportive of constructing SE databases that are to be used for terrain visualization, mobility planning, site and route selection, reconnaissance and communications planning, navigation and munitions guidance. TTD data density is generally consistent with similar portrayals on topographic line maps, terrain analysis products and hydrographic charts.

Interim Terrain Data (ITD) was designed to provide digital terrain analysis data for systems fielded before the production of Tactical Terrain Data. It consists of six thematic coverages or layers: vegetation, obstacles, transportation, and surface material, slope and drainage. Features correspond to a 1:50,000-scale map (NIMA, USAS 98a).

Vector Map (VMAP) is provided in Levels 0, 1 and 2, each increasing from small to large scale. Data coverages include boundaries, elevation, hydrography, industry, physiography, population, transportation, utilities, and vegetation. Urban Vector Map (UVMAP) provides specific vector-based geospatial data with city graphic content. The same coverages are provided as for VMAP. Detail is similar to NIMA city graphic and military city map products.

World Vector Shoreline (WVS) content includes shoreline, international boundaries, maritime boundaries and country labels. Five libraries provide data derive from 1:250,000 to 1:12,000,000 scale source. Bathymetric data is found in Digital Bathymetric Data Base (DBDB). DBDB is gridded data giving ocean depths in meters worldwide for each 5 minutes of latitude and longitude.

A primary source of terrain elevation data is NIMA's Digital Terrain Elevation Data (DTED). DTED comes in several resolutions ranging from 100 meter (Level 1) to 30 meter (Level 2) and down to 1 meter (Level 5). DTED is formatted in a uniform matrix of terrain elevation values, in 1° by 1° cells identified by southwest corner coordinates. This provides elevation data source for SE systems that require landform, slope, elevation or gross terrain roughness. While DTED is a prime source of terrain elevation data, Digital Feature Analysis Data (DFAD) is a prime source of digital feature data. DFAD is assigned an identification code and is described in terms of height, composition, length and orientation. DFAD is collected from photogrammetric as well as cartographic source material. DFAD Level 1 offers medium scale detail (1:250,000) and Level 2 offers higher scale (1:50,000). The types of features included in DFAD include roads, railways, drainage, prominent buildings in urban areas, and prominent towers and power lines.

In addition to its vector-based products, NIMA also provides other synthetic environment data in raster format. These include Arc second Raster Chart/map (ARC) Digitized Raster Graphics (ADRG) and ARC Digital Raster Imagery (ADRI). ADRG is a digital raster representation of paper cartographic products. In contrast, ADRI is produced from orthorectified panchromatic SPOT commercial imagery.

2.   NIMA's Vector Product Format Data Model

VPF was developed by NIMA as a specification for large geographic databases. The VPF data model is organized as shown in Figure 6. A VPF database is made up of libraries. Libraries are organized into coverages of thematically consistent data that share a single coordinate system and scale and that are contained within a specified spatial extent. Each coverage is then composed of features whose primitives maintain topological relationships according to one of the four levels of topology found in VPF.

VPF supports the *tiling* of coverages. Tiling is the practice of geographically subdividing coverages for the purpose of improving data management. The subdivided coverage is referred to as a tiled coverage. A tiling scheme defines tile boundaries, the size of tiles and the handling of the features that lie on tile boundaries and text primitives that cross boundaries. Tiling schemes are defined by product specifications rather than by VPF. If any of the coverages in a library are tiled, then all coverages must either use the same tiling scheme or be untiled. Edges and faces that either lie on or cross tile boundaries and connected nodes that lie on tile boundaries take part in cross-tile topology. The primitives in each tile of a tiled coverage are handled separately from primitives in other tiles. This results in each primitive having an id that is unique only within the tile. Cross-tile topology utilizes a triplet id consisting of the primitive's id in the current tile, the id of the bordering tile and the id of the continuing primitive in the bordering tile.

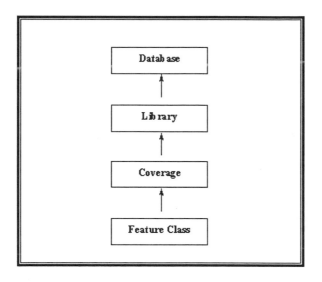

Figure 6. VPF Top Level Data Model

Five categories of cartographic features are defined in VPF: Point, Line, Area, Complex and Text. Point, Line and Area features are classified as Simple Features composed of only one type of primitive. Each Simple Feature is of differing dimensionality: zero, one and two for Point, Line and Area Features respectively. Unlike Simple Features, Complex Features can be of mixed dimensionality, and are obtained by combining Features of similar or differing dimension. The VPF feature class structural schema is shown in Figure 7 below.

The five VPF spatial primitives are:
1. *Entity node* – representing isolated features;
2. *Connected node* – endpoints defining edges;
3. *Edge* – an arc representing a linear feature or a border of a face;
4. *Face* – a two-dimensional primitive representing area features such as an area of terrain; and
5. *Text* - a cartographic primitive that allows the representation of names associated with ill-defined regions.

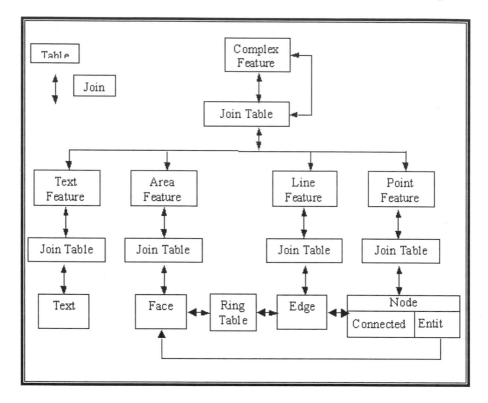

Figure 7. VPF Feature Class Structural Schema

A mandatory Minimum Bounding Box (MBB) table is associated with each edge and face primitive. The simple shape of the MBB makes it easier to handle than its corresponding primitive. The edge and face primitives have an optional *spatial index*. The spatial index is based on a binary tree, which reduces searching for a primitive down to binary search. Due to its variable length records, the connected node table has a mandatory associated *variable length index*.

VPF associates the face table with a *ring* table, which identifies the ring forming the outer boundary of each face primitive together with all internal rings of each face primitive. This table allows (along with the face table) the extraction of all of the edges that form the outer boundary and the internal rings of a face primitive. For more information, the interested reader is referred to the VPF specification (VPF 96).

VPF provides four levels of topology shown in Table 2. These range from Level 0, containing no explicit topological information, to Level 3 which explicitly represents all topological connections.

Table 2. VPF Levels of Topology. (VPF 96)

Level	Name	Primitives	Description	Example
3	Full topology	Connected nodes, entity nodes, edges and faces.	The surface is partitioned by a set of mutually exclusive and collectively exhaustive faces. Edges meet only at nodes.	
2	Planar graph	Entity nodes, connected nodes and edges.	A set of edges and nodes where, when projected onto a planar surface, the edges meet only at nodes.	
1	Non-planar graph	Entity nodes, connected nodes and edges.	A set of entity nodes and edges that may meet at nodes.	
0	Boundary representation (spaghetti)	Entity nodes and edges.	A set of entity nodes and edges. Edges contain only coordinates, not start and end nodes.	

3. Commercial Database Formats

Many commercial systems use VPF data possibly along with data from other sources such as field surveys to create 3D SE databases. Loral Advanced Distributed Simulation, Inc. (Loral), Lockheed Martin Information Systems (LMIS), Multigen, Inc., Evans & Sutherland (E&S) and Lockheed Martin Tactical Defense Systems (LMTDS) are major developers of synthetic environment database systems. Their products include database formats such as the S1000, OpenFlight, TARGET, Integrator and specific image generator formats. Some of these are described below.

The S1000 database is a Loral product. It's one of the formats used by the U.S. Army Topographic Engineering Center (TEC), Digital Products Center (DPC) to develop 3D terrain databases (Trott 96). Many other database formats are then compiled from the final S1000 database. Details of the S1000 are set forth in (Farsi 95). The S1000 is generally organized around four major blocks of data: land models (3D polygons), unique static object models (3D polygons including the geometry of buildings, trees, vehicles, targets, etc.), generic model references (2D point data), and 2D network references. The first three are organized into quadtrees, while the last is organized into a linear array of filenames, which in turn reference individual files. Features such as treelines and canopies are stored as attributed 2D vector data, that in turn is used to generate 3D polygonal geometry which conforms to the underlying terrain. Textures and generic models are stored in libraries, which are referenced by the database, but not technically part of the database. In the S1000 database, polygons are 3 or 4 sided, convex and planar, and are the lowest level geometric entity. Model polygons are stored in the local coordinate system of the model (model coordinates), while all other polygons are stored in the database's world coordinates. Among the many polygons attributes are mobility types, color, thermal properties, how it should be colored (face, vertex or textured), and shading.

LMIS's TARGET product (LMIS 99a) is organized around one or more roots, which can be either a defined 'gaming area' or a 'moving model.' The gaming area is composed of one or more 'common geographic databases' and other optional data such as a terrain grid, texture image, project control information, etc. The common geographic database is composed of one or more 'core images' and header information. Core images are in turn organized into attribute, feature and vertex tables. TARGET defines 14 different types of features, significantly more than S1000 and VPF (VPF 96). Among these are topographic polygon, topographic point and topographic line, base terrain, blended terrain and continuous terrain, terrain shadow, surface culture, radar point and radar line, and model reference. Each feature is associated with a list of vertices that define the feature. As with the S1000 database, TARGET also provides for a model library. In addition to being a database format, TARGET provides tools that enable the automated processing of standard NIMA data (such as DTED and DFAD) and of two interchange formats SIF and SEDRIS (discussed below). A toolkit also allows capture of detail from imagery and maps for inclusion within the database. When data from different sources might otherwise result in an inconsistent representation of the real world, TARGET fuses these into a consistent world model (LMIS 99b).

In contrast to S1000 and TARGET, MultiGen's OpenFlight has a much simpler database organization. OpenFlight's design, described in (Mult 96), organizes the database in a hierarchy of logical groupings. A database file header points to a 'group' or logical subset of a database. This structure allows all nodes in the group to be manipulated as a single entity. Group nodes in turn point to other groups, objects or level-of-detail nodes. Level-of-detail nodes are conceptually similar to the group node, but act as a switch to allow the display of everything below it to be turned on or off depending on range from the viewer. OpenFlight 'objects' contain a logical collection of polygons. Objects can also point to another object, to a group, to a level-of-detail node or to a polygon. The polygon, in turn, contains an ordered set of vertices, and is attributed with color, texture, materials, transparency, etc. Vertices contain a 3D coordinate and can have vertex normals and texture mapping attribution. OpenFlight also provides tools to generate terrain polygons from DTED, to convert DFAD automatically into a 3D visual scene, to construct roads, and to import SIF (discussed below) data (TEC 99). OpenFlight emphasizes visual representation, not topological relationships.

4. Three-Dimensional Data Acquisition

VPF synthetic environment related data often lacks the geometry necessary to reconstruct detailed three-dimensional objects in a 3D SE. VPF, for example, generally represents a building as a two-dimensional polygon. Much of the geometric detail and texture data necessary to reconstruct a realistic-looking 3D building that closely resembles its real-world counterpart is omitted.

There is on going research into the automated extraction of this type of 3D feature data from imagery. Many of these methods use photogrammetric techniques such as shadow analysis and line-corner analysis to automate the identification and extraction of 3D man-made features from high-resolution imagery (Irvin 89, Roux 94). In addition to establishing the geo-location and the shape of the features, heights can be approximated, and the results can be used to generate 3D views. More recent work has made use of a combination of data from airborne laser scanning, color imagery and high-resolution 2D maps (Haala 99a, Haala 99b). Other efforts are devoted to developing fully textured 3D models of features from digital video imagery (Geometrix 2000).

Many 3D models are created for SEs using packages such as TARGET (LMIS 99b) and OpenFlight (MULT 96). Digitized building blueprints, when available, can provide highly accurate 3D structural detail in a relatively short period of time.

4. THE SYNTHETIC ENVIRONMENT DATABASE GENERATION PROCESS

NIMA produces its VPF formatted synthetic environment data in segmented thematic coverages. This data organization generally follows historic mapping techniques of organizing data in disjoint thematic layers, which are overlaid to produce the desired map view of the world. In contrast, the development of a realistic detailed SE requires the integration of these data sources and considerable data processing. DTED, DFAD and ITD, for example, are produced by different processes from different sources, and do not always correlate very well (Trott 96). Transportation networks, buildings and other 3D features must be integrated with 3D terrain elevation data to produce 3D synthetic environment databases. Roads, for example, existing only as one-dimensional features in VPF must be widened to their real-world width, and simply draping roads over 3D terrain does not assure a reasonable pitch (Abdelguerfi 97).

Specific approaches to the creation of a SE may vary based on available tools, system requirements, application specific needs, etc. The process basically follows the flow chart shown in Figure 8 below and can be described in terms of data collection, terrain skin creation, model creation and data integration. This is described in detail in (Abdelguerfi 97, Abdelguerfi 98, Mamaghani 98, Trott 96) and will only be outlined here.

DATA COLLECTION: Data collection involves identification and collection of relevant data such as DTED, DFAD, ITD, etc. It also involves supplementing NIMA digital data with digital imagery and cartographic data as may be necessary. In addition, where NIMA data may lack the necessary attribution (such as real-world appearance of a point feature), on-site surveys may be necessary.

TERRAIN MODEL CREATION: Terrain models typically fall into one of three categories: Grid, Triangulated Irregular Network (TIN) or Constrained TIN. The Grid model utilizes a rectangular grid with the data points at the intersection of the grid intervals used to identify terrain elevation. Elevation values must be interpolated in the event no values coincide with the grid intervals. A higher data density (or finer mesh) is required to achieve precision with rough surfaces. Grid models cannot accurately represent surface features that are smaller than the given point spacing of the grid. With a 250-meter wide grid interval, for example, a 50-meter wide feature must either be omitted or must be represented as 250 meters wide. A TIN, in contrast, approximates the surface by means of a network of planar, non-overlapping and irregularly shaped triangular facets, with the vertices of each triangle located at the data elevation points (Floriani 87). They can approximate any surface at any level of accuracy with a minimal number of polygons (Scarlatos 90). A constrained TIN is constructed by using significant line segments obtained from feature data in the triangulation process. The line segments can be part of a significant surface feature such as a building footprint, transportation network or lakeshore, and are considered to have reliable elevation attributes. This assures, for example, that roadways will have reasonable pitch, that buildings will not float above the terrain or be buried beneath it and that waterway surfaces will have uniform elevation.

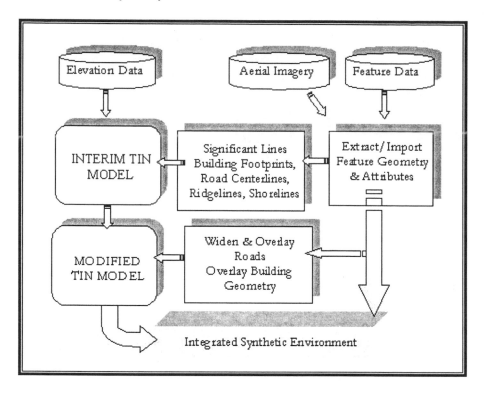

Figure 8. Flow Chart of 3D Synthetic Environment Creation

GENERIC/SPECIFIC 3D MODEL CREATION: VPF data provides at most two-dimensional symbolic representation of features (VPF 96). This requires that three-dimensional models be imported from already existing sources, constructed as specific replications of features or constructed as generic feature models. For example, a bridge may be represented as a line in VPF with attribution indicating that it is a bridge. A polygon may be used for the representation of the footprint of a building, with attributes such as height and building composition. Figure 9 shows an example of a typical 2D symbolic representation of the building as might be found in a VPF database alongside a 3D model of the same building as might be found in a 3D SE.

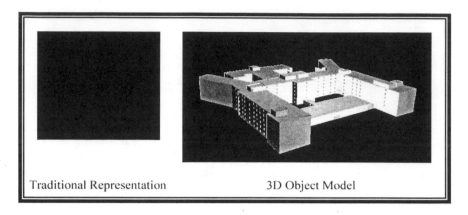

Figure 9. Two Views of the U.S. Public Health Service Hospital located at the Presidio, San Francisco, California (Ladner 2000)

DATA INTEGRATION: In addition to constructing three-dimensional models, feature data may also have to be conformed to the underlying terrain. This may involve integrating the feature models with the terrain skin, translating the models to the correct location, or thinning features that are too numerous for the scale of the SE. Edge matching may also be an issue, as feature data obtained from different coverages may not have consistent edge information. Realistic texture or color may also be applied.

5.   SYNTHETIC ENVIRONMENT DATABASE EXCHANGE, RE-USE AND SHARING

SE databases are costly and time consuming to produce, and there are many proprietary data models and formats in use. The ability to reuse data from existing SE databases to build new SE databases for new applications is desirable. Data repositories and database interchange specifications are two means of accomplishing this.

1.   Data Repositories

Data repositories and clearing houses hold SE data in a centralized location or make the availability of data at different locations known to prospective users. Such data sources include the Terrain Resource Repository (TRR), the Master Environmental Library (MEL), the Tactical Oceanography Wide Area Network (TOWAN), the National Geospatial Data Clearinghouse (NGDC), and the National Oceanographic and Atmospheric Administration Server (NOAA).

The TRR is maintained by NIMA's Terrain Modeling Project Office (TMPO). The TRR provides Internet access to various terrain data products available from the Department of Defense (TMPO 2000). Users can access samples of many of NIMA's standard data products, along with software for viewing. The TRR also provides links to numerous web sites that are sources for environment data. Among these are data sources maintained by state agencies, the U.S. Geologic Survey, the National Oceanographic and Atmospheric Administration, the U.S. Census Bureau, the U.S. Department of Transportation, the U.S. Department of Agriculture, the Bureau of Land Management, the Canadian Government, and the United Nations.

The Defense Modeling Simulation Office (DMSO) maintains MEL. MEL indexes environmental data source location. Through MEL, users can locate and order SE data online (MEL 2000).

TOWAN is provided by the Naval Research Laboratory at Stennis Space Center as an online environmental data repository and server that allows Department of Defense personnel and their contractors to search for and retrieve environmental information. TOWAN makes oceanographic databases available, including bathymetric, geoacoustics, ice and magnetics. TOWAN is one of the nodes in MEL (TOWAN 2000).

The NGDC aggregates over 100 spatial data servers and provides a search interface. Search options include location, time period of content, full text and fielded search using country names or U.S. placenames. A custom search allows users to define parameters including map, temporal and server (NGDC 2000).

The NOAA Server provides an on-line search by area-of-interest access to several databases. These databases include the NOAA Central Library, the Japan Science and Technology Corporation, the Foreign Data Library, the Office of Oceanographic and Atmospheric Research, the National Weather Service, and the National Snow and Ice Data Center (NOAA 2000).

2. Interchange Specifications

While centralized data repositories and clearing houses afford the means of making the existence of synthetic environment data known to prospective users, data interchange specifications resolve some of the problems that may arise from importing that data into the user's native format. Two such specifications are the Standard Simulator Database (SSDB) Interchange Format (SIF), also known as Project 2851 (SIF 93) and the Synthetic Environment Database Specification and Interchange Specification (SEDRIS) (SEDRIS 2000). SEDRIS, for example, specifies a data model, which defines a standard representation of the SE and serves as an intermediary between the major existing proprietary products by providing an API for exporting to and importing from and from those products.

3.   Distributed Simulations of Synthetic Environments

While tools such as SEDRIS have been developed in order to foster the interchange of SE data, other technologies exist that enable distributed simulations of synthetic environments. These include Distributed Interactive Simulation and High Level Architecture (Dahmann 99, Davis 95, Hofer 95, and HLA 98). These technologies establish connectivity between independent workstations to create a consistent SE with respect to perception and behavior. Distributed interactive simulations of SEs have been noted to be beneficial to training. Trainees can interact together in a common synthetic environment space. Insights can be gained about processes involving human interactions, behavior and decision making. Although distributed interactive simulation technologies have primarily evolved in the M&S arena, they may prove to benefit any distributed simulation application whether it involves training, research, prototyping products, etc.

6.   SYNTHETIC ENVIRONMENT VISUALIZATION TECHNOLOGIES

This section reviews some of the existing technology used for visualizing SEs. These typically provide the user with some degree of immersion into the environment depending on the application. That may involve a computer screen display in which the user can *walk* across the terrain or *drive* an automobile on a real-world highway, or it may involve some of the more sophisticated immersive technologies discussed below. For added realism, the SE may provide sounds appropriate to the environment being modeled or provide haptic devices to give the user a physical sense of *touching* an object he is virtually touching through interaction with the SE.

1.   The CAVE

The CAVE Automatic Virtual Environment, Figure 10, is a fully immersive projective system composed of a room constructed of large rear-projection screens on which graphics can be projected on the surfaces. A tracking system tracks the user's head and hand orientation and position. Users wear stereo shutter glasses. As the viewer moves inside the CAVE, the correct stereoscopic perspective projections are calculated based on the viewer's position (Pape 97).

Figure 10. View of the CAVE (FSI 2000)

2. The Workbench

Also known as the Responsive Workbench or the Immersadesk, this device is a semi-immersive projective system based on a high-resolution tabletop display. Three-dimensional SEs are projected as stereoscopic images onto the surface of a table. As with the Cave, viewers wear stereo shutter glasses and a tracking device, which calculates the correct perspective image for each viewer's location. Tracking may be by way of magnetic, infrared or an inertial system. Interaction with the environment is by way of a stylus and gloves, each also equipped with special tracking devices. Systems enabling two-handed manipulations, shown in Figure 11, are possible (Cutler 97).

Figure 11. View of the Workbench (Cutler 97)

3.   Head Mounted Displays

Head Mounted Displays (HMDs), Figure 12, fix monitors in front of the eyes usually blocking all views of the user's surroundings. When equipped with a tracking device, the user's view changes to a new perspective as he or she turns his or her head or moves forward/backward, providing a more interactive visual display.

Figure 12. View of a Head Mounted Display (LIC 2000)

4.   Virtual Retinal Display

Figure 13 shows an example of the Virtual Retinal Display (VRD), which projects electronic information on the eye without the use of a screen. The image is conveyed by scanning an electronically encoded beam of light through the pupil to the retina. The user has the impression of viewing a high quality video image an arm's length away. VRD technology can be incorporated into a variety of small hand-held or head-worn devices. This technology has the advantage of not obstructing the user's view of his/her natural surroundings (Virre 98).

5.   Monitors

Computer monitors may use more advanced stereoscopic techniques, but may also employ various software packages to enhance the normal two-dimensional windows. These rendering packages include OpenGl, Java3D, the Virtual Reality Modeling Language, Iris Performa, OpenInventor, etc.

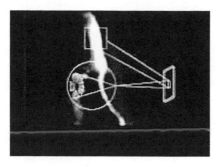

Figure 13. Virtual Retinal Display (MSVI 2000)

6. Haptics

Haptics provide a realistic sense of touch to users of SEs. Incorporated into gloves, haptics correlate what the user sees in the SE with what he should feel by providing a feedback stimulus to the user. Sandia National Lab's Cyberglove shown in Figure 14, for example, tracks the user's hand movements and finger orientation. It provides tactile sensations through vibrations transmitted by way of plungers within the glove that tap the user's fingertips (Villarreal 99).

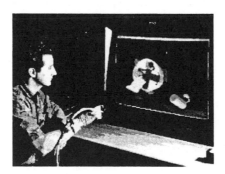

Figure 14. Sandia National Lab's Cyberglove (Villarreal 99)

7. CONCLUSION

This chapter has introduced three-dimensional synthetic environments by examining their uses, data sources, databases, database exchange mechanisms, distributed architectures and visualization technologies. These topics have been addressed from the standpoint of the 3D SE as a digital representation of the natural environment. While 3D SEs have traditionally been associated with military M&S, they are being used in such diverse disciplines as education, urban planning and manufacturing. Although much synthetic environment source data is produced by the National Imagery and Mapping Agency, the process of constructing a 3D SE database is often a time consuming and costly process. The use of clearing houses and interchange specifications to exchange and re-use 3D SE databases is therefore desirable. Visualization of SEs can involve sophisticated devices such as the CAVE, Workbench or head mounted display, all providing the user with a sense of immersion into the environment, or merely a computer monitor running a 3D graphics program.

8. ACKNOWLEDGMENTS

The authors thank the National Imagery and Mapping Agency and the U.S. Marine Corps Warfighting Lab for their sponsorship of this research.

Abdelguerfi, M., Cooper, E., Wynne, C., Shaw, K. (1997). *An Extended Vector Product Format (EVPF) suitable for the representation of three-dimensional elevation in terrain databases*, Int. J. Geographical Information Science, Vol. 11, No. 7, pp. 649-676.

Abdelguerfi, M., Ladner, R., Shaw, K. (1998). *Terrain Database Generation*, 1998 American Society for Photogrammetry and Remote Sensing Annual Conference, Orlando, Florida, pp.129-138.

Birkel, P.A. (1997). *SEDRIS Geospatial Reference Model*, http://www.sedris.org, July 10.

Cutler, L.D., Frohlich, B., Hanrahan, P. (1997). *Two Handed Direct Manipulation on the Responsive Workbench*, Proceedings of the Symposium on Interactive 3D Graphics, ACM SIGGRAPH, pp. 107-114.

Dahmann, J.S. (1999). *High Level Architecture for Simulation*, Defense Modeling and Simulation Office, Presentation.

Daimler Chrysler (1999). http://www.daimlerchrysler.de/.

Davis, P.K. (1995). *Distributed Interactive Simulation in the Evolution of DoD Warfare Modeling and Simulation*, Proceedings of the IEEE, Vol. 83, No. 8, pp. 1138-1155.

Department of Defense (1995). *Modeling & Simulation Master Plan*, DoD 5000.59-P.

Evans and Sutherland (1999). http://www.evansandsutherland.com/.

Floriani, L. (1987). *Surface Representations Based on Triangular Grids*, The Visual Computer, Vol. 3, 1987, pp. 27-50.

Fakespace Systems, Inc. (2000).

Geometrix, Inc. (2000). http://www.geometrixinc.com/.

Haala, N. and Walter, V. (1999a). Automatic Classification of Urban Environments for Database Revision using Lidar and Color Aerial Imagery. Joint ISPRS/EARSEL Workshop, Valladolid, pp. 76-82

Haala, N. and Brenner, C. (1999b). Virtual City Models from Laser Altimeter and 2D Map Data. Photogrammetric Engineering & Remote Sensing, Vol. 65, 7, pp. 787-795.

IEEE P 1516.1. (1998). *HLA Interface Specification, Draft 1.*

Hofer, D.C., Loper, M.L. (1995). *DIS Today*, Proceedings of the IEEE, Vol. 83, No. 8, pp. 1124-1137.

Irvin, R.B. and McKeown, Jr., D.M. (1989). *Methods for Exploiting the Relationship Between Buildings and Their Shadows in Aerial Imagery*, IEEE Transactions on Systems, Man, and Cybernetics, Vol. 19, No. 6.

Koninger, A. and Bartel, S. (1998). *3D-GIS for Urban Purposes*, GeoInformatica, Vol. 2, No. 1, pp. 79-103.

Ladner, R., Abdelguerfi, M., and Shaw, K. (2000). *3D Mapping of an Interactive Synthetic Environment*, Computer, Vol. 33, No. 3, pp. 35-39.

Liquid Image Corporation (2000)). http://www.liquidimage.ca/.

Liggett, R., Friedman, S., Jepson, W. (1995). *Interactive Design/Decision Making in a Virtual Urban World: Visual Simulation and GIS*, Proceedings of the Fifteenth Annual ESRI User Conference. Palm Springs, CA.

Lockheed Martin Corporation (1999a). *Advanced Distributed Simulation Technology II (ADST II) Target/Sedris API (DO #0043) CDRL AB02 Sedris Mapping Document*, Lockheed Martin Information Systems, ADST II, P.O. Box 780217, Orlando, FL 32878, 1999.

Lockheed Martin Corporation (1999b). *Compu-Scene TARGET*, Lockheed Martin Information Systems, http://www.lmco.com/lmis/level4/target.html.

Loftin, R.B. (2000). *Hands Across the Atlantic*, NASA/Johnson Space Center and University of Houston, reported at http://www.vetl.uh.edu/sharedvir/handatl.html.

Loftin, R.B. (1998). *Distributed Virtual Environments for Collective Training*, Proceedings of the 1998 Image Conference, pp. RB1 - RB6.

Mamaghani, F. (1998). *Digital Illusion: Creation and Use of Synthetic Environments in Realtime Networked Interactive Simulation*, Clark Dodsworth, Jr., Contributing Editor, ACM Press, pp. 99-114.

Master Environment Library (2000). Defense Modeling & Simulation Office, http://mel.dmso.mil.

Microvision, Inc. (2000). http://www.mvis.com/default.htm,.

OpenFlight Scene Description, MultiGen, Inc. (1996). 550 S. Winchester Blvd., Suite 500, San Jose, CA 95128, Version 14.2.4, Revision A.

Federal Geographic Data Committee (FGDC) National Geospatial Data Clearinghouse (NGDC) (2000). http://www.fgdc.gov.

National Imagery and Mapping Agency (NIMA). *Digitizing the Future*.

National Oceanographic and Atmospheric Administration (2000). http://www.esdim.noaa.gov/noaaserver-bin/NOAAServer.

Ota, D., Loftin, B., Saito, T., Lea, R., and Keller, J. (1998). *Virtual Reality in Surgical Education*, Virtual Environment Technology Laboratory, University of Houston, http://www.vetl.uh.edu/surgery/vrse.html, 1998.

Pape, D., Cruz-Neira, C., Czernuszenko, M. (1997). *The CAVE User's Guide*, Electronic Visualization Laboratory, University of Illinois at Chicago, 851 S. Morgan St., Room 1120, Chicago, IL 60607-7053.

Roux, M., and McKeown, D.M. (1994). *Feature Matching for Building Extraction from Multiple Views*, Proceedings of the IEEE Conference on Computer Vision and Pattern Recognition, pp. 46-53.

Scarlatos, L. and Pavlidis, T. (1990). *Hierarchical Triangulation Using Terrain Features*, IEEE Conference on Visualization, pp.168-174.

Schmieder, H. (1998). *Requirements for Virtual Reality Systems in Driving Simulation*, Proceedings of the 1998 Image Conference, pp. HJ1-HJ8.

SEDRIS (2000). http://www.sedris.org.

Department of Defense (1993). *Standard Simulator Data Base (SDDB) Interchange Format (SIF) Design Standard*, MIL-STD-1821.

TEC (1999). *Commercial Terrain Visualization Software Product Information*, U.S. Army Topographic Engineering Center, http:\\www.tec.army.mil/TD/tvd/survey/MultiGen.html.

Tempfli, K. (1997). Urban 3D Topologic Data and Texture by Digital Photogrammetry, Proceedings of the American Society for Photogrammetry and Remote Sensing, pp. 952-963.

Tactical Oceanography Wide Area Network (2000). Naval Research Laboratory, Stennis Space Center, http://www7180.nrlssc.navy.mil/homepages/TOWAN/TOWAN.htm.

Terrain Resource Repository, Terrain Modeling Project Office (2000). http://www.tmpo.nima.mil/mel.

Trott, K. (1996). *Analysis of Digital Topographic Data Issues in Support of Synthetic Environment Terrain Data Base Generation*, TEC-0091, U.S. Army Corps of Engineers, Topographic Engineering Center.

U.S. Army Simulation, Training, and Instrumentation Command (1998a). Orlando, Florida, *SEDRIS and The Synthetic Environment Domain, Volume 1 of the SEDRIS Document SET*, 12350 Research Parkway, Orlando, FL.

U.S. Army Simulation, Training, and Instrumentation Command (1998b). Orlando, Florida, *Synthetic Environment Data Representation and Interchange Specification Overview, Volume 2 of the SEDRIS Documentation Set*, 12350 Research Parkway, Orlando, FL.

Virtual Environment Technology Laboratory (1998). University of Houston, Project Science Space, http://www.vetl.uh.edu/ScienceSpace/ScienceSpace.html, 1998.

Villarreal. Q. and Venkatesan, P. (1999). *Virtual Reality*, Sandia National Laboratories, http://www.ca.sandia.gov/VR/.

Virre, E., Pryor, H., Nagata, S. and Furness, T.A. (1998). *The Virtual Retinal Display: A New Technology for Virtual Reality and Augmented Vision in Medicine*. In Proceedings of Medicine Meets Virtual Reality, San Diego, California, USA, Amsterdam: IOS Press and Ohmsha, pp. 252-257.

Department of Defense, *Interface Standard for Vector Product Format* (2000). MIL-STD.

Chapter 2

Multiresolution Modeling Of Three-Dimensional Shapes

Leila De Floriani, Paola Magillo

Affiliation Dipartimento di Informatica e Scienze dell'Informazione,Università di Genova, Via Dodecaneso, 35, 16146 Genova, ITALY, Email: {deflo,magillo}@disi.unige.it

Key words:	Multiresolution, decomposition-based representations, geometric meshes, selective refinement.

Abstract:	Multiresolution models can provide representations of a geometric shape at different degrees of accuracy and complexity, based on user requirements. They have an impact in many applications, which require the manipulation of complex three-dimensional objects. In this chapter, we present a survey of existing multiresolution techniques. A comprehensive framework for multiresolution modeling is introduced, and existing models are presented, interpreted and compared by referring to such framework.

1. INTRODUCTION

Manipulation of models of complex three-dimensional shapes is common in computer graphics and virtual reality, computer-aided-design, geographic information systems, medicine, etc.

In this chapter, we deal with geometric models based on spatial decompositions, also known as *geometric meshes*. A mesh is an aggregate of a finite number of basic entities, called *cells*. When a mesh is used to describe the shape of an object, each cell represents a portion of the object. The resolution of a mesh is related to the density of its cells, and it is a fundamental parameter for the accuracy of the object representation. Accurate representations need high resolutions, and, thus, a high number of cells, which leads to high costs for managing the mesh.

Three-dimensional models are either fully synthetic or obtained from sampling physical objects. In both cases, the models produced by modern tools for either 3D acquisition and reconstruction, or computer-aided shape design, become more and more accurate, with larger and larger sizes.

Models at high resolution can provide very accurate object representations, but they can easily become too large to be effectively used in tasks such as rendering, recognition, classification, collision detection, and manipulation planning. This problem cannot be simply solved by using more powerful machines, since, while hardware and software technology improves, the resolution of geometric models that we are able to construct increases at an even faster rate.

However, most applications tasks do not need a high resolution in *each parts* of an object, at *all times*. Thus, we can reduce memory and computational costs by using *selectively refined* meshes, i.e., meshes whose resolution is variable in space according to specific application requirements. The basic idea is balancing the accuracy in the representation with the constraints imposed by an application and/or the software and hardware platform. For instance, in rendering a scene, the resolution needed in different parts of the objects depends on the distance of such parts from the viewpoint, since many details are required only close to the observer. In an interactive visualization program with a moving viewpoint, the resolution of the meshes to be rendered should be dynamically adapted.

Generating meshes at variable resolution is crucial for real-time visualization and animation of large CAD models (e.g., aircrafts, ships, buildings) used in virtual reality. The possibility of reasoning at different levels of abstraction on the shape of an object helps operations such as collision detection (to quickly solve trivial cases on a coarse representation) and editing (to edit an intermediate resolution and then propagate the modifications to a representation at full resolution). In finite element analysis, for an efficient solution of an equation, the density of the mesh must reflect the expected behavior of the solution, being higher where the solution changes more rapidly. A multiresolution model of the domain allows the extraction of different resolutions without computing them from scratch. The possibility of traversing several and increasing levels of resolution helps processing spatial interference queries since an initial raw solution may be computed with little computational effort and then refined locally.

In principle, selectively refined meshes could be computed on-line from a reference mesh at the highest available resolution, by using *mesh simplification algorithms* available at the state of the art. But this approach is unfeasible in practice, because of the high costs of such algorithms.

Multiresolution models permit to decouple the simplification phase from the selective refinement phase. A multiresolution model is a comprehensive structure which organizes several representations of a shape at different resolutions. Such models are based on a mesh simplification process that is performed once to build the model off-line, and the intermediate phases of such process are encoded within the model.

Multiresolution models allow adapting the resolution of a geometric model to application needs in order to trade off accuracy of representation and use of memory and processing time. A multiresolution mesh can be seen as a *black box* that can be queried for obtaining selectively refined meshes on-the-fly, according to user requirements. Multiresolution models can also act as *spatial indexes*, since they encode connections between representations of the same spatial location at increasing resolution and complexity. Such connections can be traversed in a coarse-to-fine direction in order to answer spatial queries.

This chapter covers existing multiresolution models for representing three-dimensional objects. A comprehensive framework for multiresolution modeling is introduced, and existing models are presented, interpreted and compared by referring to such framework. The chapter is organized as follows. Section 2 provides some background notions. Section 3 introduces our general framework for multiresolution meshes. In Section 4, existing multiresolution models are reviewed and interpreted based on the general framework of Section 3. Finally, Section 5 contains some concluding remarks.

2. PRELIMINARIES

We deal with the representation of *solid objects* in space. A solid object is a subset of E^3 which is *bounded, connected, closed*, and *regular*. Intuitively, regularity means that the object is fully three-dimensional and does not contain "dangling" segments or surfaces). Figure 1 shows some subsets of E^3 which are, or are not, solid objects.

Another common requirement is the boundary surface to be a *two-manifold*. This means that any point on the surface has a neighborhood that is topologically equivalent to an open disk. In Figure 1, the boundary of solid (b) is not a two-manifold because of the presence of edge *e*.

Some models have been developed to represent *terrains*. Terrains can be viewed as special objects where just the upper surface of the object is relevant for modeling, and this surface is monotonic with respect to the *xy*-plane. For this reason, terrains are sometimes called *two-and-half-dimensional objects*.

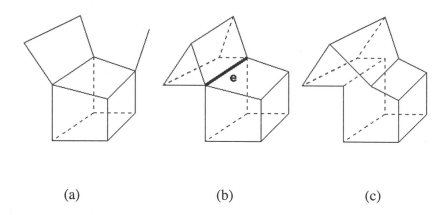

(a)   (b)   (c)

Figure 1. Set (a) is not a solid object since it is not regular (it contains dangling lower-dimensional parts); sets (b) and (c) are solid objects; but only set (c) has a two-manifold boundary.

We consider geometric models based on *spatial decompositions*, also called *meshes*. In this approach, the shape of a given object is described as an aggregate of a finite number of basic elements, called *cells*. Cells have a predefined, simple shape that can be described with a fixed and restricted number of parameters. Usually, they are polygons with a predefined number of vertices (either quadrilaterals or triangles).

A *mesh* is a collection of cells with the following properties:
1. two distinct cells have disjoint interiors;
2. the union of all cells covers the boundary surface of a solid object.

In many applications, spatial decompositions are used in which the boundaries of two cells that touch each other are matching. In this case, we have the following additional property:
3. if two distinct cells touch, then the intersection of their boundaries consists of edges which are common to both cells.

Such spatial decompositions are called *conforming*. Figure 2 shows a conforming mesh and a mesh that is not conforming.

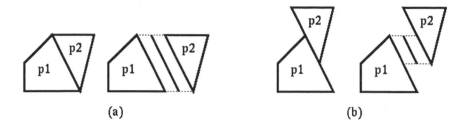

Figure 2. *Possible situations for two neighboring cells p_1 and p_2 in a mesh (the exploded view of the two cells with their intersection segment is shown on the right). Mesh (a) is conforming, while (b) is not conforming because the intersection between the boundaries of p_1 and p_2 is not an edge of either of them.*

Conforming meshes have several advantages. First of all, they have a well-defined combinatorial structure, in which each cell is adjacent to exactly one cell along each of its edges. This is important for designing data structures, for navigating the model (e.g., neighbor finding) and when defining *functions* over the cells of the spatial decomposition, as explained later.

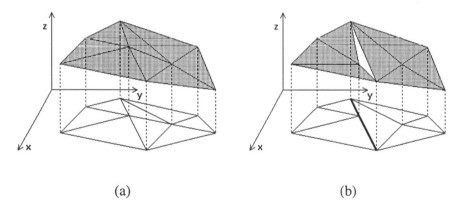

Figure 3. *Terrain models based on a planar triangle mesh with linear interpolating functions. The mesh in (b) is not conforming (note the vertical crack in the surface over the thick edge).*

A decomposition-based geometric model consists of a mesh, which provides a description of the object shape. In some cases, a function can be piecewise defined over the cells of the mesh in order to provide a more appropriate shape representation. For instance, a triangle mesh can be used as a basic shape representation, while higher order functions can be defined on the triangles of the mesh in order to get a smooth surface. Another example is terrain representation. A terrain model consists of a mesh covering a planar domain, while the object surface is obtained by projecting the cells of such decomposition into three-dimensional space based on the elevation values known at their vertices (see Figure 3).

When defining functions over the cells of a triangle mesh, the continuity of the resulting surface is ensured only if triangles match along their edges, i.e., if the mesh is conforming. If the given decomposition is not conforming, then the resulting three-dimensional surface may present discontinuities (see Figure 3 (b)).

3.   MULTIRESOLUTION MESHES

A multiresolution model encompasses the range of resolutions between a mesh at the lowest resolution and a mesh at the highest resolution. In fact, such models are built through iterative processes that either refine a low-resolution mesh, or coarsen a high-resolution mesh. The basic idea behind any multiresolution model is collecting the modifications performed on the mesh during construction and organizing them by defining suitable dependency relations. Dependency relations drive the extraction of meshes at intermediate resolutions, possibly variable in space. Moreover, such relations also allow traversing the model from low to high resolution, thus providing a spatial index associated with the model.

The various models proposed in the literature differ in:
- the process of refinement or simplification used to build the model, and, in particular, on the *type of modifications* used;
- the way in which *relations* among modifications are *defined*;
- the *data structure* used to encode the modifications and their relations, its space complexity, the *algorithms* operating on it, and their computational cost.

In general, modifications with a small extension in space, and a loose notion of dependency, enhance the capability of a model in providing a wide range of intermediate resolutions, including resolutions variable in space. On the other hand, the type of modifications and the notion of dependency used in a model must obey some rules in order to ensure the consistency of the meshes that can be retrieved.

A key point is whether arbitrary meshes can be extracted from the model, or only meshes that are guaranteed to be conforming. Another important distinction is between models that can provide meshes at various resolutions, but all uniform in space, and models that support true selective refinement, with the possibility of extracting meshes at variable resolution.

Moreover, several models in the literature are described through the data structure representing them, while only a few models are presented at a higher level of abstraction.

In this section, we introduce a general framework for multiresolution meshes that:
-   is independent of the specific type of modification since it defines the constraints that a modification must undergo to produce a correct result when applied to a [conforming] mesh;
-   considers a loose notion of dependency just in order to ensure the correctness of [conforming] meshes extracted from the multiresolution model.

1. Modifications of a Mesh

Given a mesh S, a sub-mesh S' of S is a subset of its cells. The boundary of a sub-mesh S' is the set of cell edges which divide a cell of S' from a cell of $S \setminus S'$.

We define a *modification* of a mesh S as a pair of meshes (S_1, S_2), where (i) S_1 is contained into, or equal to S, and (ii) S_2 and $S \setminus S_1$ do not intersect $S \setminus S_1$ except possibly at their boundaries (see Figure 4). The intuitive idea is modifying S by replacing S_1 with S_2.

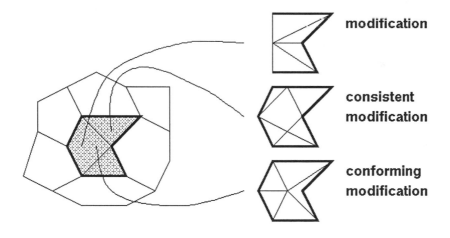

Figure 4. Possible types of modifications of a given mesh.

Typical modification operators used in existing multiresolution models are:

1. The *quadtree rule*, for regular meshes of quadrilaterals, which replaces a square cell with four squares obtained by splitting it in the center of the square (see Figure 5 (a)).
2. The *rule of quaternary triangulations*, which replaces a triangle with four triangles obtained by joining the midpoints of its edges (see Figure 5 (b)). This type of modifications applies to regular triangle meshes.
3. The *bisection rule for right triangles*, replacing a right triangle with two right triangles obtained by splitting it through the middle point of its longest edge (see Figure 5 (c)).
4. The *insertion of a vertex* in an irregular mesh of triangles. Inserting a vertex deletes one or more triangles which form a connected set. The triangles which are deleted depend on the specific algorithm used. A typical example is vertex insertion in a planar triangulation based on the Delaunay criterion. The hole left by the removed triangles is filled with new triangles obtained by joining the new vertex inserted with each vertex of the polyline bounding the hole (see Figure 5 (d)).
5. The *deletion of a vertex* from an irregular mesh of triangles. This is symmetric with respect to vertex insertion. The deletion of a vertex removes the triangles incident in it. The deletion of such triangles from the mesh leaves a hole bounded by a polyline. New triangles are created which fill the hole, by using just the vertices of the polyline (see Figure 5 (e)).
6. *Edge collapse*, which operates on irregular mesh of triangles and shrinks an edge to a vertex. The two triangles incident in the edge become two segments, and the surrounding triangles are deformed accordingly (see Figure 5 (f) and (g)). The edge may collapse to one of its endpoints, or to a new vertex located on the edge (e.g., its middle point). Note that an edge collapse of the first type can be regarded as a special case of vertex deletion.

Other modification operators reduce to repeated applications of the above ones. For instance, *triangle collapse* contracts a triangle to a vertex and deforms the mesh consequently, which can be reduced to a pair of edge collapses.

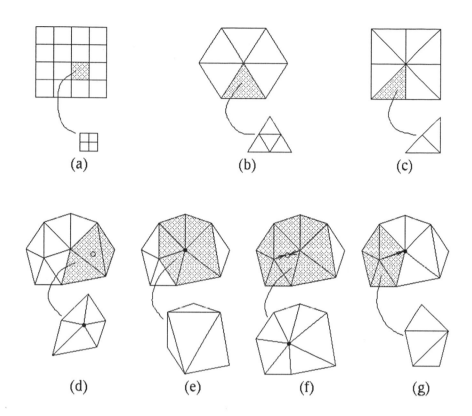

Figure 5. Some modification operators: (a) quadtree; (b) quaternary triangulation; (c) bisection of right triangles; (d) vertex insertion; (e) vertex deletion; (f) edge collapse to a middle point; (g) edge collapse to one endpoint.

A modification of a mesh S is called *consistent* if the boundary shared by $S \setminus S_1$ and S_1 is the same (as a point set) as the one shared by $S \setminus S_1$ and S_2 (see Figure 4). Intuitively, in a consistent modification, S_2 fills the hole left in S after the removal of S_1.

A modification is called *conforming* if it is consistent, and the boundary portions shared by $S \setminus S_{\_1}$ consist of the same set of edges as those shared by $S \setminus S_1$ and S_2 (see Figure 4).

All existing models use consistent modifications, but not all of them use conforming modifications. Vertex insertion and deletion, as well as edge collapse are examples of conforming modifications.

If we apply a conforming modification to a conforming mesh, the result is still a conforming mesh. On the contrary, a modification that is just consistent does not preserve the conformity of the given mesh.

2. Batches of Modifications

During a process of mesh refinement or mesh coarsening, an initial mesh undergoes a sequence of modification steps. A batch of modifications corresponds to the idea of *one step* of the process, which executes either one, or a set of independent modifications simultaneously (i.e., modifications which do not interfere with each other).

More precisely, we say that two [consistent] conforming modifications (S_1,S_2) and (S'_1,S'_2) of a mesh S are *independent* if S_1 and S'_1 are disjoint (as cell sets), and their union $(S_1 \cup S'_1, S_2 \cup S'_2)$ is a consistent [conforming] modification.

A *batch of modifications* on a conforming mesh S is a set of mutually independent modifications which are consistent conforming and are all applied to S at the same time. Figure 6 shows a sequence of batches applied to a mesh. A batch can also contain just one modification.

 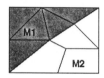 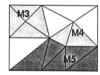 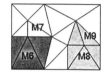

Figure 6. A sequence of three batches refining an initial mesh. Modifications within the same batch are highlighted with different colors.

Now, we introduce our definition of *dependency* between modifications. Suppose we apply a sequence of batches to a mesh. Let M_1 and M_2 be two modifications belonging to different batches, such that the batch of M_1 precedes the one of M_2 in the sequence. We say that M_2 *directly depends* on M_1 if M_2 removes some cell inserted by M_1 and not yet removed (and reinserted) in any other batch in between. For instance, in Figure 6, modification M_3 depends on M_1, while M_4 and M_5 depend on M_2. Modification M_6 depends on M_1 and M_5. The transitive closure of the relation of direct dependency is a *partial order*.

3. A Framework for Multiresolution

Consider a process that starts with an initial mesh Σ_{low} at low resolution and progressively refines it into a final mesh Σ_{high} at high resolution, by performing a sequence of modifications (equivalently, one may think to progressively coarsen Σ_{high} into Σ_{low} through a reversed sequence of modifications). A multiresolution model records the modifications performed during this process and the dependency relations among them.

We represent graphically the set of modification involved in a process of mesh refinement / simplification, along with their dependency relations, as a Directed Acyclic Graph (DAG) in which the nodes represent modifications, and the arcs represent links of direct dependency among modifications. By convention, arcs are directed from the coarser to the finer resolution. We call this DAG a *multiresolution mesh*. Figure 7 shows the multiresolution mesh for the refinement process of Figure 6.

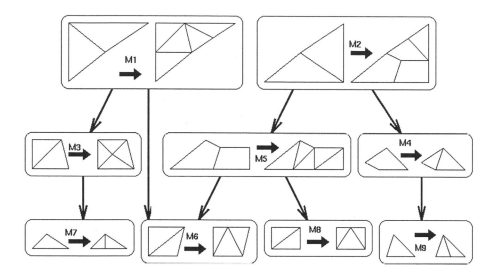

Figure 7. The DAG of the multiresolution mesh defined by the modifications of Figure 6.

The multiresolution mesh provides all meshes that can be obtained by using some of the modifications performed during the process of mesh refinement / simplification. When extracting a representation of a shape, the idea is executing just the modifications which are necessary to refine the shape where needed and to the required resolution. Dependency links will enforce the execution of some other modifications as well to maintain mesh correctness.

A subset of the nodes of the DAG is called *closed* if, for each node in the set, all parents are in the set. A closed subset of nodes corresponds to a set of modifications that can be applied to the initial mesh while respecting the dependency relation. Closed subsets are in one-to-one correspondence with all the meshes that can be obtained from the multiresolution mesh. Figure 8 shows a closed subset of nodes and its mesh.

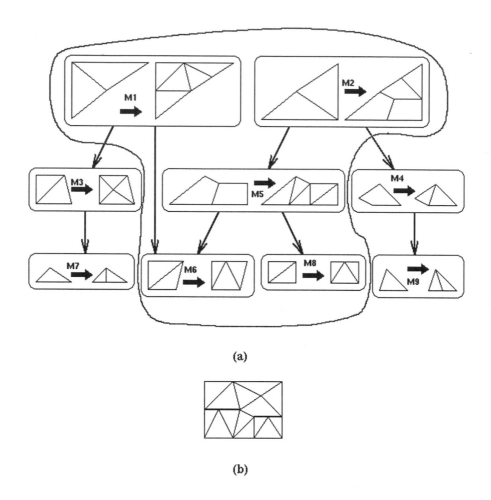

(a)

(b)

Figure 8. (a) A closed subset of nodes in the multiresolution mesh of Figure 7, and (b) the corresponding mesh. Note that the mesh in (b) is not conforming (the thick segments have one cell on one side and two cells on the other side).

Note that the meshes obtained in this way are, in general, not conforming (see Figure 8 (b)), with the exception of the case in which all modifications are themselves conforming.

In order to characterize the collection of all the conforming meshes obtainable from a model, we introduce the concept of *cluster*. Clusters allow aggregating several non-conforming modifications into a conforming one.

Consider a set of modifications $\{M_1,...M_k\}$ belonging to the same batch. We say that the set $\{M_1...M_k\}$ is a *cluster* if the union of modifications $M_1...M_k$ is a conforming modification, and no other proper subset of

{M₁...Mₖ} has such property. In Figure 6, modifications M_6 and M_7 form a cluster, and modifications M_8 and M_9 form another cluster. Each of the other modifications forms a singleton cluster.

Consider two clusters C_1 and C_2 belonging to distinct batches, where the batch of C_1 precedes that of C_2. We say that C_2 depends on C_1 if some modification in C_1 depends on some modification in C_2 .

We define a second DAG, called a *conforming multiresolution mesh* that captures the dependency relation between the clusters of the process. Note that a cluster is necessarily a conforming modification.

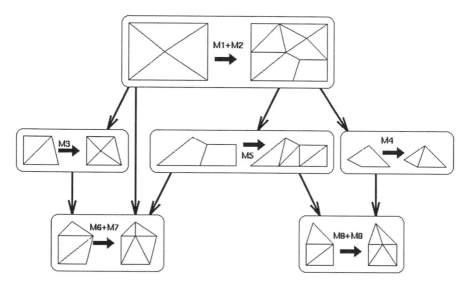

Figure 9. The DAG of the conforming multiresolution mesh for the modifications of Figure 6.

In the conforming multiresolution mesh, the nodes represent the clusters, and the arcs represent links of direct dependency among clusters. Figure 9 shows the conforming multiresolution mesh for the refinement process of Figure 6: the conforming multiresolution mesh is obtained from the multiresolution mesh by merging some of its nodes, namely those nodes corresponding to modifications that belong to the same cluster.

If, in all batches, all modifications are conforming, then each cluster contains just one modification, and the multiresolution mesh is the same as the conforming multiresolution mesh.

Closed subsets of nodes are defined on the conforming multiresolution mesh in the same way. Through its closed sets, the conforming multiresolution mesh gives us all *conforming* meshes that can be obtained from the model.

4.   SURVEY OF EXISTING MODELS

In this section, we review multiresolution models proposed in the literature within the framework defined in Section 3. We classify existing multiresolution models in the following three types:
- *layered models*, which encode just a sequence of unrelated meshes at increasing resolutions;
- *nested models*, based on the containment of a set of cells at high resolution into one cell at low resolution;
- *evolutionary models*, in which cells belonging to consecutive resolutions may overlap properly.

The only meshes which can be obtained from layered models are the ones belonging to the given sequence, thus there is no possibility of selective refinement. Such models are standard technology in graphics languages and packages, such as OpenInventor™ (OpenInventor, 1994; Wernecke, 1994), and VRML (VRML, 1996), and are used to improve efficiency of rendering: depending on the distance from the observer, one of the available meshes is selected. Layered models are of limited interest and will not be treated further. The other two classes of models are described in the following subsections in detail.

1.   Nested Models

Nested models are based on modifications that operate within each cell independently and refine it locally into a mesh. They can be represented as a tree in which each node corresponds to a mesh that covers one of the cells of its parent node. The nested structure makes these models very effective as spatial indexes.

Nested models have been developed to represent two-and-half dimensional objects, like terrains, where the nested mesh is used to decompose the planar domain. Arbitrary surfaces can be treated with these models provided that they are first split into patches, in such a way that each patch can be considered two-and-half dimensional.

Most nested models require data with a *regular distribution in space* and are based on the subdivision a square or a triangle into scaled copies of it, according to a predefined pattern.

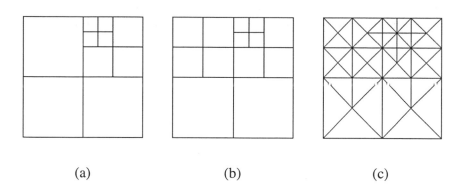

(a)   (b)   (c)

Figure 10. (a) A non-conforming mesh from a quadtree, (b) balancing the subdivision, (c) triangulation giving a conforming mesh.

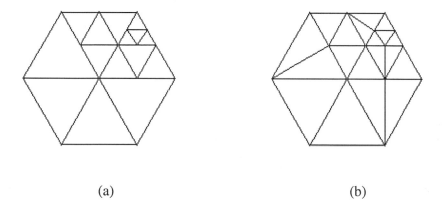

(a)   (b)

Figure 11. (a) A non-conforming mesh from a quaternary triangulation; (b) the same mesh made conforming through subdivision.

The *quadtree* (Samet, 1990) recursively subdivides a square into four quadrants. The *quaternary triangulation* (Gomez and Guzman, 1979; Dutton, 1996) is a generalization of the quadtree to a triangular grid: it recursively subdivides a triangle into four equal triangles. Both models can be represented as a quaternary tree. Quadtrees and quaternary triangulations can provide conforming meshes at uniform resolution, corresponding to one layer in the tree, while meshes at variable resolution, which combine cells from different layers, are inherently non-conforming (see Figure 10 (a) and 11 (a)).

A proposal to overcome the problem of non-conforming meshes is the *restricted quadtree* (Von Herzen and Barr, 1987). A restricted quadtree is essentially a quadtree in which adjacent leaves are allowed to differ for no more than one level; leaves are triangulated according to predefined patterns in order to achieve conformity: a quadrant is subdivided into four right triangles by its diagonals, and each such triangle is further subdivided into two right triangles by joining the center of the quadrant with the opposite edge, only if the quadrants adjacent along such an edge are at a deeper level than the current quadrant (see Figure 10). Restricted versions of quaternary triangulations have also been proposed (Gross et al., 1997) (see Figure 11 (b)).

An alternative view of restricted quadtrees considers the whole hierarchy as formed by right triangles. *Hierarchies of right triangles* (Lindstrom et al., 1996; Evans et al., 1997) recursively bisect a right triangle into two right triangles through the insertion of a new vertex in the middle of its longest edge. The corresponding containment hierarchy can be represented as a binary tree. Alternatively, the model can be seen as based on replacing pair of right triangles, adjacent along their longest edge, with four right triangles (Lindstrom et al., 1996; Evans et al., 1997). In this view, the model is better represented as a directed acyclic graph in which each node has exactly two parents and four children (Duchaineau et al., 1997; Pajarola, 1998). Hierarchies of right triangles can support the extraction of conforming meshes both at a uniform and at a variable resolution (see Figure 10 (c)). The conforming meshes at variable resolution which can be obtained from a hierarchy of right triangles are the same as the ones obtained from restricted quadtrees.

Regular nested models can be encoded by extremely compact and efficient data structures, because both the modifications and the nesting relation are implicitly defined on the basis of fixed patterns. As an example, Lindstrom et al., 1996 implement a hierarchy of right triangles by storing only the raw grid of vertices, while both the triangles and the tree are implicitly provided.

Regular nested models can be interpreted within the framework presented in Section 3. Modifications are just consistent, but not conforming. Starting with a single cell, each batch refines all cells of the current mesh simultaneously. The tree describing the nesting relation is the same as the multiresolution mesh. Clusters for the conforming multiresolution mesh can be constructed in the following way:

- For quadtrees and quaternary triangulations, each batch is one cluster. The corresponding conforming multiresolution mesh is structured as a sequential list (see Figure 12). The closed subsets of nodes are in one-to-one correspondence with batches, and give only meshes at uniform resolutions.

- For hierarchies of right triangles, clusters are formed by pairs of modifications. The corresponding conforming multiresolution mesh is a DAG in which each node has two parents and four children (see Figure 13). Closed sets of nodes give meshes at variable resolution, and they are exponential in the number of batches. Hierarchies of right triangles also provide a characterization of all conforming meshes which can be extracted from a restricted quadtree.

–

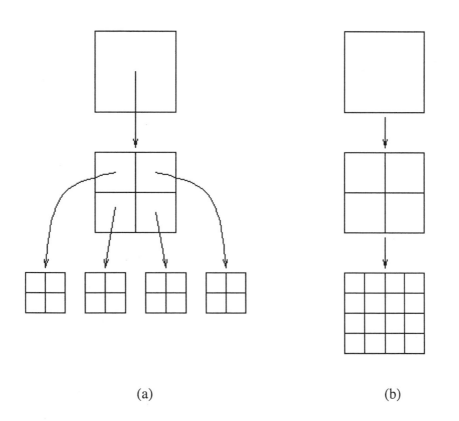

(a)   (b)

Figure 12. (a) The multiresolution mesh and (b) the conforming multiresolution mesh for a quadtree.

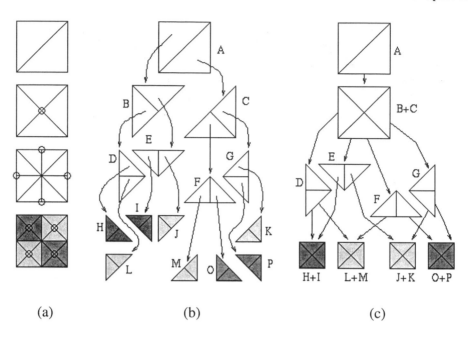

(a)   (b)   (c)

Figure 13.   (a) The batches, (b) the multiresolution mesh and (c) the conforming multiresolution mesh of a hierarchy of right triangles.

In the literature, nested models suitable for data with an irregular distribution, have also been proposed, based on irregular triangulations (Scarlatos and Pavlidis, 1992; De Floriani and Puppo, 1995). Here, conformity is achieved by using a different strategy for refining triangles. These models are built through refinement. Each batch of the refinement process corresponds to a certain threshold applied to the approximation error. In a batch, every triangle is refined by inserting a non-fixed number of points, which may lie in its interior or on its edges, until the approximation error is lower than a predefined threshold for that batch. Unlike quadtrees and quaternary triangulations, an edge may survive across different levels, and thus the edges which are not refined in a batch can divide the batch into several clusters. In nested irregular triangulations, modifications are consistent, but not conforming. The tree describing the nesting relation is the same as the multiresolution mesh.

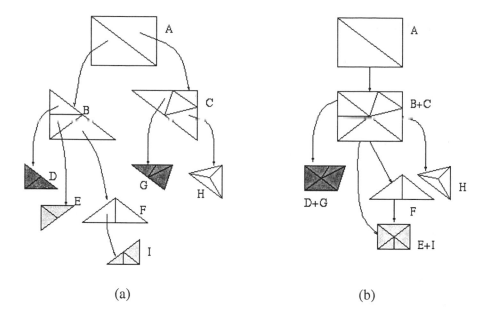

(a)   (b)

Figure 14 (a) The multiresolution mesh and (b) the conforming multiresolution mesh for an irregular nested model.

Each pair of modifications in a batch, which refine the same edge, belongs to the same cluster (see Figure 14). The extension of clusters depends on how many edges are refined in a single batch, which in turns depends on the construction algorithm, and on data configuration. Few refined edges give small clusters, and thus many meshes at variable resolution can be extracted from the corresponding conforming multiresolution mesh, but extracted meshes tend to contain slivery triangles.

2. Evolutionary Models

Existing evolutionary models deal with scattered data and are based on irregular triangle meshes. Modifications used in these models affect a set of neighboring cells in a mesh. Evolutionary models are built through a refinement process based on vertex insertion (De Floriani, 1989; Bertolotto et al., 1990; Klein and Straßer, 1997; Cignoni et al., 1997) or through a coarsening process using vertex removal (Schroeder et al., 1992; De Berg and Dobrindt, 1995, Bajaj et al., 1996), edge collapse (Hoppe, 1996; Luebke and Erikson, 1997; Duchaineau et al., 1997; Guéziec et al., 1998; Kobbelt et al., 1998), or triangle collapse (Hamann, 1994, Gieng et al., 1997).

All such types of modifications are conforming. Therefore, the multiresolution mesh is the same as the conforming multiresolution mesh. The number of closed sets of nodes in the multiresolution mesh (and, thus, the number of meshes available from the model) depends on the heuristics used in the construction process. An analysis in this perspective, for models based on vertex deletion, can be found in De Floriani et al., 1997. In models built through coarsening, modifications are performed one at a time, or a batch of independent modifications is applied simultaneously (De Berg and Dobrindt, 1995 , Xia et al., 1997). In models built through vertex insertion, it is difficult to design independent modifications as the extension of a modification is known only after performing it.

Batches of independent modifications lead to models with a more balanced structure which is especially relevant when using the model as a spatial index. Some models are built by deleting vertices with a bounded degree, or edges with a bounded number of triangles incident in their endpoints. This guarantees that the overall number of cells in the model is bounded by a linear function of the number of cells in the mesh at the highest resolution.

Several evolutionary models (and thus the data structures used to store them) are based on notions of dependency different from the one defined in Section 3. This may prevent the extraction of certain meshes, or allow the extraction of meshes that may not be correct, since they come out from modifications that are not applied in the same conditions in which they were applied during construction.

In describing evolutionary models, we distinguish between models that encode a *sequence of modifications*, models based on edge collapse which encode a *forest of vertices* plus additional dependency links, and models are based on other approaches.

2.1   Sequential Models.

Sequential models consider modifications sorted in a total order that reflects the order in which they have been applied during construction.

In Bertolotto et al., 1995; Cignoni et al., 1997 , the change in resolution of a mesh during a monotonic process of mesh refinement is traced by assigning a *life* to each cell (note that the same can be done in mesh coarsening). The life of a cell is the range of resolutions at which the cell appears in the mesh.

The model stores all the cells which have appeared during the process, each tagged with its life. Life of cells is used as a filter to obtain meshes at a uniform resolution. The mesh for a given uniform resolution is formed by the collection of all cells that contain such value in their lives. The model does not support selective refinement.

Other sequential models store a coarse mesh plus a sorted sequence of modifications that progressively refine it. Such models allow for very compact data structures, since all modifications in the sequence belong to a predefined type, and thus can be described through a few parameters. Models of this type have been proposed based on edge collapse (Hoppe, 1996), vertex insertion (Klein and Straßer, 1997), and triangle collapse (Gieng et al., 1997).

It is quite straightforward to extract one of the meshes appeared in the construction process: we scan the list of modifications and perform modifications from the list, until we reach the desired resolution. Meshes at variable resolution can be extracted by scanning the list of modifications and applying only the ones that refine the portions of the object where a more detailed representation is needed. Unfortunately, a single scan of the list is not sufficient, since a modification that needs to be performed may depend on some earlier modification that has been skipped. To avoid such problem, dependency links are computed on-the-fly with complex and computationally expensive algorithms (Hoppe, 1996; Klein and Straßer, 1997).

2.2 Vertex Forests.

In the literature, several models have been proposed which are built through a coarsening process based on edge collapse, and encoded as *vertex forests*. The primary structure of such models is a binary forest of vertices, where the children of a vertex v , created by collapsing an edge e, are the two endpoints v_1, v_2 of e (see Figure 15). Vertices of the original mesh are the roots of the forest.

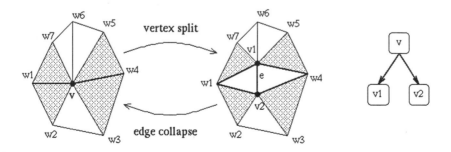

Figure 15 Edge collapse with its reverse edge split, and the corresponding forest branch.

If we think about a vertex (node of the forest) as the modification that creates such vertex through edge collapse, we see that this forest encodes a subset of the dependency relations between modifications. It is easy to verify that the modification collapsing e to v depends on the modifications that introduced v_1 and v_2 (by collapsing other two edges).

As the binary forest does not capture all dependency relations of the multiresolution mesh, the various models define extra dependency links between vertices of the forest, which are stored separately.

Xia et al., 1997 store a link from a vertex v to each of the vertices $w_1,...,w_k$ that are adjacent to at least one of the two endpoints of the edge e that is collapsed to v during the construction process (see Figure 15). Their idea is that the modification collapsing e to v depends on the collapses that generate $w_1,...,w_k$. This captures all dependency relations of the multiresolution mesh, but also stores a few redundant links.

Hoppe, 1997 links a vertex to six of the vertices $w_1,...,w_k$ that are adjacent to the endpoints of edge e that was collapsed to v . These six vertices are the vertices of the four triangles adjacent to the two triangles that are collapsed to segments when e is collapsed to v (the triangles shown in grey in Figure 15). However, this does not capture all the existing dependencies, and there are still redundant links in the structure.

Luebke and Erikson, 1997 keep just the binary forest of vertices, and ignore all other dependencies.

Guéziec et al., 1998 store vertex dependencies explicitly by means of a DAG, but they consider dependencies as in Xia et al., 1997, thus their DAG contains some redundant arcs with respect to our multiresolution mesh.

The model proposed by El-Sana and Varshney 1999 is based on edge collapse of the type that shrinks an edge to an *internal* point. It stores the binary forest of vertices plus a vertex enumeration that allows finding all dependencies between modifications on-the-fly. This results in a very compact data structure. Vertices are numbered during the process of iterative edge collapse: the n vertices of the original mesh at high resolution are numbered arbitrarily from 1 to n; the remaining vertices are numbered with consecutive numbers as they are created.

Given a mesh corresponding to a closed subset of modifications, the following rules define the acceptable transformations of the current mesh:
− an edge e can be collapsed if and only if all vertices adjacent to the endpoints of e have a number lower than the vertex v resulting from the collapse;
− a vertex v can be expanded into an edge if and only if all vertices adjacent to v have a number lower than v.

Dependency links defined in this way cover all links present in the multiresolution mesh, plus some redundant links. This approach does not work for edge collapses that collapse an edge to one of its endpoints.

The problem of redundant dependency links is intrinsic of these models, since the binary forest of vertices may contain parent-child links that correspond to a path, rather than to a single arc, in our multiresolution mesh. But such extra links do not compromise the integrity of the model. On the contrary, in models in which some dependency links are missing, any extracted set of cells is guaranteed to be a conforming mesh, but it may contain triangles which were not present in the original sequence of meshes generated during the construction of the model.

2.3   Other Approaches.

The Multi-Triangulation (MT) (Puppo, 1998; De Floriani et al., 1999; Magillo, 1999) is a model that can be constructed with any process of refinement or coarsening using *conforming modifications*, and is a direct instance of the (conforming) multiresolution mesh considered here. Implementations of the MT are discussed in De Floriani et al., 1997.

The *Hyper-Triangulation* (Cignoni et al., 1997) can be viewed as a model that encodes dependencies between conforming modifications by reducing them to adjacency relations between the involved triangles. The idea is better explained by thinking that, for each modification (S_1, S_2), the triangles of S_2 are pasted over the triangles of S_1 by glueing the two sets along their common boundary polyline, thus forming a sort of bubble. The data structure stores all triangle-triangle adjacencies in this arrangement of bubbles. It has been shown in Magillo 1999 that such structure can be regarded as an indirect representation of the DAG of a (conforming) multiresolution mesh. The extraction of meshes at variable resolution is efficient only in the special case in which resolution monotonically increases with the distance from a given reference point.

5.   CONCLUSIONS

In this chapter, we have described a general framework for multiresolution representation of three-dimensional shapes based on geometric meshes, which consists of a a partially ordered set of modifications refining an initial mesh. Meshes at variable resolution can be obtained by selecting a subset of modifications consistent with the partial order. This framework encompasses all existing multiresolution models and helps understanding the number and the properties of meshes that a model can provide.

In this chapter, we have considered meshes with just two-dimensional cells, but the framework proposed here can be extended to regular meshes in three and higher dimensions in a straightforward way (see Magillo, 1999). On the other side, in some applications it is important to deal with non-regular shapes, and with modifications that change the dimensionality of (portions of) a shape. Extensions of the framework in such a direction will be the subject of our future research.

Bajaj, C., Bernardini, F., Chen, J., and Schikore, D. (1996). Automatic reconstruction of 3D CAD models. In Strasser, W., Klein, R., and Rau, R., editors, *Theory and Practice of Geometric Modeling*. Springer-Verlag.

Bertolotto, M., De Floriani, L., and Marzano, P. (1995). Pyramidal simplicial complexes. In *Proceedings 4th International Symposium on Solid Modeling*, pages 153-162, Salt Lake City, Utah, U.S.A. ACM Press.

Cignoni, P., Puppo, E., and Scopigno, R. (1997). Representation and visualization of terrain surfaces at variable resolution. *The Visual Computer*, 13:199-217.

De Berg, M. and Dobrindt, K. (1995). On levels of detail in terrains. In *Proceedings 11th ACM Symposium on Computational Geometry*, pages C26-C27, Vancouver (Canada). ACM Press.

De Floriani, L. (1989). A pyramidal data structure for triangle-based surface description. *IEEE Computer Graphics and Applications*, 8(2):67-78.

De Floriani, L., Magillo, P., and Puppo, E. (1997). Building and traversing a surface at variable resolution. In *Proceedings IEEE Visualization 97*, pages 103-110, Phoenix, AZ (USA).

De Floriani, L., Magillo, P., and Puppo, E. (1999). Multiresolution representation of shapes based on cell complexes. In *Proceedings International Conference on Discrete Geometry for Computer Imagery*, Esiee, Noisy-le-Grand, France.

De Floriani, L. and Puppo, E. (1995). Hierarchical triangulation for multiresolution surface description. *ACM Transactions on Graphics*, 14(4):363-411.

Duchaineau, M., Wolinsky, M., Sigeti, D., Miller, M., Aldrich, C., and Mineed-Weinstein, M. (1997). ROAMing terrain: Real-time optimally adapting meshes. In *Proceedings IEEE Visualization'97*, pages 81-88.

Dutton, G. (1996). Improving locational specificity of map data - a multiresolution, metadata-driven approach and notation. *International Journal of Geographic Information Systems*, 10(3):253-268.

El-Sana, J. and Varshney, A. (1999). Generalized view-dependent simplification. *Computer Graphics Forum*, 18(3):C83-C94.

Evans, W., Kirkpatrick, D., and Townsend, G. (1997). Right triangular irregular networks. Technical Report 97-09, University of Arizona.

Gieng, T., Hamann, B., Joy, K., Schussman, G., and Trotts, I. (1997). Constructing hierarchies of triangle meshes. *IEEE Transactions on Visualization and Computer Graphics*, 4(2):145-160.

Gomez, D. and Guzman, A. (1979). Digital model for three-dimensional surface representation. *Geo-Processing*, 1:53-70.

Gross, M., Staadt, O., and Gatti, R. (1996). Efficient triangular surface approximations using wavelets and quadtree data structures. *IEEE Transactions on Visualization and Computer Graphics*, 2(2):130-144.

Guéziec, A., Taubin, G., Lazarus, F., and Horn, W. (1998). Simplicial maps for progressive transmission of polygonal surfaces. In *Proceeding ACM VRML98*, pages 25-31.

Hamann, B. (1994). A data reduction scheme for triangulated surfaces. *Computer Aided Geometric Design*, 11(2):197-214.

Hoppe, H. (1996). Progressive meshes. In *ACM Computer Graphics Proceedings*, Annual Conference Series (SIGGRAPH '96), pages 99-108.

Hoppe, H. (1997). View-dependent refinement of progressive meshes. In *ACM Computer Graphics Proceedings*, Annual Conference Series, (SIGGRAPH '97), pages 189-198.

Klein, R. and Strasser, W. (1997). Generation of multiresolution models from CAD data for real time rendering. In Klein, R., Strasser, W., and Rau, R., editors, *Theory and Practice of Geometric Modeling (Blaubeuren II)*. Spinger-Verlag.

Kobbelt, L., Campagna, S., Vorsatz, J., and Seidel, H. (1998). Interactive multi-resolution modeling of arbitrary meshes. In *Comp. Graph. Proc., Annual Conf. Series (SIGGRAPH '98)*, ACM Press.

Lindstrom, P., Koller, D., Ribarsky, W., Hodges, L., Faust, N., and Turner, G. (1996). Real-time, continuous level of detail rendering of height fields. In *Comp. Graph. Proc., Annual Conf. Series (SIGGRAPH '96)*, ACM Press, pages 109-118, New Orleans, LA, USA.

Luebke, D. and Erikson, C. (1997). View-dependent simplification of arbitrary polygonal environments. In *ACM Computer Graphics Proceedings, Annual Conference Series, (SIGGRAPH '97)*, pages 199-207.

Magillo, P. (1999). Spatial Operations on Multiresolution Cell Complexes. PhD thesis, Dept. of Computer and Information Sciences, University of Genova (Italy).

OpenInventor Architecture Group (1994). *Inventor Mentor: OpenInventor Reference Manual*. Addison Wesley.

Pajarola, R. (1998). Large scale terrain visualization using the restricted quadtree triangulation. In *Proceedings IEEE Visualization'98*, pages 19-24, Research Triangle Park, NC. IEEE Comp. Soc. Press.

Puppo, E. (1998). Variable resolution triangulations. *Computational Geometry Theory and Applications*, 11(3-4):219-238.

Samet, H. (1990). *Applications of Spatial Data Structures*. Addison Wesley, Reading, MA.

Scarlatos, L. and Pavlidis, T. (1992). Hierarchical triangulation using cartographics coherence. *CVGIP: Graphical Models and Image Processing*, 54(2):147-161.

Schroeder, W., Zarge, J., and Lorensen, W. (1992). Decimation of triangle meshes. In Catmull, E. E., editor, *ACM Computer Graphics (SIGGRAPH '92 Proceedings)*, volume~26, pages 65-70.

Von Herzen, B. and Barr, A. (1987). Accurate triangulations of deformed, intersecting surfaces. *Computer Graphics (SIGGRAPH 87 Proceedings)*, 21(4):103-110.

VRML (1996). *The Virtual Reality Modeling Language Specification - Version 2.0.*

Wernecke, J. (1994). *The Inventor Mentor: Programming Object-Oriented 3D Graphics with Open Inventor*. Addison Wesley.

Xia, J., El-Sana, J., and Varshney, A. (1997). Adaptive real-time level-of-detail-based rendering for polygonal models. *IEEE Transactions on Visualization and Computer Graphics*, 3(2):171-183.

Zorin, D., Schroeder, P., and Sweldens, W. (1997). Interactive multiresolution mesh editing. In *Comp. Graph. Proc., Annual Conf. Series (SIGGRAPH '97)*, ACM Press, pages 259-268.

Chapter 3

Adding The Third Dimension To Digital Mapping

Miyi Chung, Dr. Roy Ladner, Ruth Wilson, John Breckenridge, Kevin B. Shaw
Naval Research Laboratory

Key words: Synthetic environment, 3D-GIS, VRML, VPF extension, VPF+, non-manifold, 3D topology

Abstract: The Digital Mapping, Charting & Geodesy Analysis Program (DMAP) at the Naval Research Laboratory has been developing the distribution of geographic data over the Web through its Geospatial Information Database. While this work has primarily included digital mapping information from a variety of formats, DMAP has also been working on 3D synthetic environment data delivery. This chapter describes DMAP's work to provide a three-dimensional representation of geographic data. We provide an overview of the data structures used to reconstruct 3D synthetic environments and to store full 3D topology. We also describe a prototype that supplements traditional 2D digital-mapping output with a 3D interactive synthetic environment.

1.   INTRODUCTION

With the increasing use of computers, mapping has grown from paper charts and maps to digital format. The Digital Mapping, Charting and Geodesy Analysis Program (DMAP) at the Naval Research Laboratory has been actively involved in this area through its Geospatial Information Database (GIDB). The GIDB is an object-oriented, CORBA compliant spatial database that supports remote access and analysis of spatial data via a Java Applet over the Internet (GIDB). The digital maps produced by the GIDB like their paper counterparts, however, omit much geometric and visual information available in a three-dimensional synthetic environment

(3D SE). In contrast to the 2D digital map, the 3D SE also provides a virtual world that the user can explore. Our synthetic environment work has focused on developing a 3D-application prototype that would assist the U.S. Marine Corps with mission preparation and rehearsal and also provide onsite awareness during actual field operations in urban areas. Because these operations require practice in physically entering and searching both entire towns and individual buildings, we designed a prototype that supplements the more traditional 2D digital-mapping output with a 3D interactive synthetic environment.

Our prototype uses an extension of the National Imagery and Mapping Agency's (NIMA) Vector Product Format (VPF) (VPF 96), known as VPF+ (Abdelguerfi 98). The representational scheme of VPF+ includes topologic information in addition to geometric information. The geometric information allows for detailed 3D modeling. The topologic information encompasses the adjacencies involved in 3D manifold and non-manifold objects, and is described using a new, extended Winged-Edge data structure. This data structure is referred to as "Non-Manifold 3D Winged-Edge Topology," and it adds a new level of topology to VPF called Level 4 Full 3D Topology (Level 4). The inclusion of explicit topological information about three-dimensional relationships in the environment means that many 3D spatial relationships do not have to be derived at run-time, a factor that should be significant to many applications.

2.   THE VPF+ DATA STRUCTURE

NIMA has promulgated VPF as a government standard for large geographic databases. Some of NIMA's VPF products, for example, include Urban Vector Map, Digital Nautical Chart, Tactical Terrain Data and Digital Topographic Data. These databases are numerous. VPF+ was designed as a superset of the VPF specification to afford VPF users a smooth transition to 3D within the traditional VPF paradigm.

1.   VPF+ Primitives

The data structure relationships of VPF+ are summarized in the object model shown in Figure 1. References to geometry are omitted for clarity. There are five main VPF+ primitives found in Level 4 topology:
- *Entity node* – used to represent isolated features.
- *Connected node* – used as endpoints to define edges.
- *Edge* – an arc used to represent linear features or borders of faces.

- *Face* – a two-dimensional primitive used to represent a facet of a three-dimensional object such as the wall of a building.
- *Eface* – describes a use of a face by an edge.

Unlike the topology of traditional VPF, Level 4 topology does not require a fixed number of faces to be incident to an edge. The *Eface* is a new primitive that is introduced to resolve some of the ensuing ambiguities. Efaces describe a use of a Face by an Edge and allow maintenance of the adjacency relationships between an Edge and zero, one, two or more Faces incident to an Edge. This is achieved in VPF+ by linking each edge to all faces connected along the edge through a circular linked list of efaces. Figure 2, for example, shows three faces incident to a single edge, three efaces and three "next" edges. Each eface, as shown in Figure 2, identifies the face it is associated with, the next eface in the list and the "next" edge about the face in relation to the edge common to the three faces. Efaces are also radially ordered in the linked list in a clockwise direction about the edge in order to make traversal from one face to the radially closest adjacent face a simple list operation.

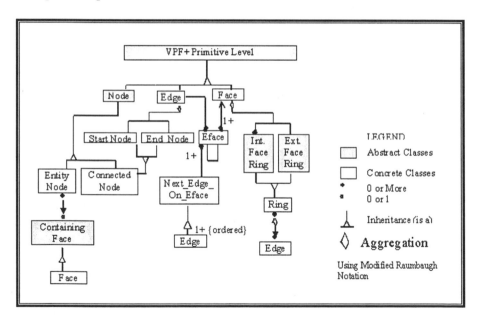

Figure 1. VPF+ Primitive Level Object Model

1.1   VPF Enhancements

In addition to the eface structure, VPF+ introduces several extensions to VPF consistent with non-manifold topology and 3D modeling.   One extension is the Node-Edge relationship. VPF relates each Connected Node to exactly one Edge. VPF+ allows for non-manifold Nodes. This requires that a Node point to one Edge in each object connected solely through the Node and to each dangling Edge (an edge that is adjacent to no face). This relationship allows for the retrieval of all Edges and all Faces in each object and the retrieval of all dangling Edges connected to the Node.

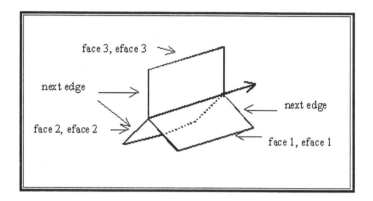

Figure 2. Relationship of a Shared Edge to its Faces, Efaces and Next Edge

Another extension is the absence of VPF's Universal Face in the non-manifold 3D topology. The "universe face" is defined in VPF as the unbounded region surrounding a coverage. A coverage in VPF is composed of features whose primitives maintain topological relationships according to one of the four levels of topology (Levels 0 through 3) found in VPF. The universal face is absent in Level 4 since it is a planar construct and Level 4 topology deals with 3D features.

A third extension provided by VPF+ is the presence of Two-Sided Faces. Faces are defined in VPF as purely planar regions. In VPF+ Faces may be one sided or two sided. A two sided Face, for example, might be used to represent the wall of a building with one side used for the outside of the building and the other side for the inside of the building. Feature attribute information would be used to render the two different surface textures and color. A one sided Face might then be used to represent the terrain surface.

Embedded faces are another extension offered by VPF+. That is, faces may be embedded within a 3D object. As an example, an embedded double-sided Face might divide a building into two floors. Other double-sided Faces might then divide each floor into separate rooms.

Another extension provided by VPF+ is Object Orientation. Orientation of the interior and exterior of 3D objects is organized in relation to the normal vector of Faces forming the surface boundary of closed objects. This allows for easy distinction between an object's interior and exterior.

VPF organizes spatial data into coverages of thematically consistent data that share a single coordinate system and scale and that are contained within a specified spatial extent. Each coverage is then composed of features whose primitives maintain topological relationships according to one of the four levels of topology (Levels 0 through 3) found in VPF. VPF+ extends this with Level 4 topology, which supports a single, integrated, topologically consistent three-dimensional coverage of heterogeneous features. This environment can include objects generally associated with the terrain surface (buildings and roads for example). It can also include objects that are not attached to the terrain but are rather suspended above the terrain surface or below a water body's surface.

1.2 Non-Manifold Objects

Topology is significant to many applications. Modeling and simulation applications, for example, make use of dynamic, reasoning software models that utilize non-visual spatial information about the environment (USAS 98). Non-manifold objects are commonplace in the real world and should also be readily found in 3D SEs. Explicitly maintaining non-manifold topology should eliminate the need to computationally derive many spatial relationships at run-time.

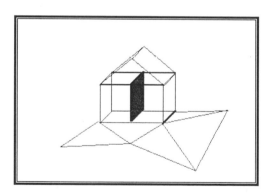

Figure 3. Non-Manifold Condition with Multiple Faces Incident at a Single Edge

Some examples of non-manifold objects are shown in Figures 3 through 5. Figure 3 gives an example of a building (shown in wireframe for clarity) with an interior face representing an interior wall and a portion of a terrain surface shown in wireframe. Each of the four edges defining the interior face is adjacent to exactly three faces - the interior face and two each for the faces forming the front and rear walls, ceiling and floor of the building. Additionally, each horizontal edge forming the baseline of the faces which makes up the exterior walls of the building is adjacent to three faces - one forming a terrain triangle, one representing the building's floor and one representing the building's exterior wall.

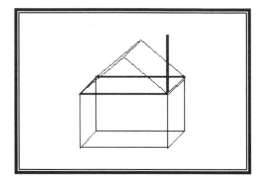

Figure 4. Non-Manifold Condition Consisting of Dangling Edge

Figure 4 shows another example of a non-manifold condition that may be found in a 3D SE. The wireframe building has an edge attached at the roof. The edge, which may represent an antenna, is a dangling non-manifold edge since it is adjacent to no face.

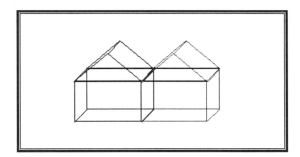

Figure 5. Two Buildings Sharing a Face With a Non-Manifold Condition at the Shared Face

A final example of a non-manifold condition that may be found in a 3D SE is shown in Figure 5. There, two buildings are shown sharing a common face. At least one non-manifold condition is identified by the red edge, which is related to five faces - the shared face forming the common wall, two ceiling faces and two roof faces.

3. THE PROTOTYPE

The prototype consists of a Web-based virtual reality application for a Military Operations in Urban Terrain (MOUT) site at Camp Lejeune, North Carolina. The MOUT site consists of a small city built by the U.S. Marine Corps for the purpose of training in an urban setting. This application employs a Web browser to select a user-defined extent of terrain and known features existing within that extent. The database is queried and a 2D map is produced alongside a 3D synthetic environment generated using the Virtual Reality Modeling Language (VRML). A Web-browser plug-in such as Cosmo Player provides interactive 3D functionality such as the capability for the user to move through and interact with the SE.

We created a 3D synthetic environment for this prototype that replicates its real-world counterpart by including natural features as well as man-made structures such as buildings, roads, and streetlights. The elevation data for the MOUT site is Digital Terrain Elevation Data (DTED), Level 5, with one-meter resolution. We used ArcInfo to create a Triangulated Irregular Network (TIN) of the elevation data. The original terrain elevation data contained over 90,000 elevation points for an area of only approximately 600 meters square. TINning reduced the total elevation points to approximately 400, greatly improving performance. The remaining elevation points were considered adequate to approximate the terrain since this geographic area is known to be relatively flat. Lines forming the buildings' footprints were used as constraints to guarantee a uniformly flat terrain under each of the buildings. As a final terrain data preprocessing step, ArcInfo was used to convert the TIN into an ArcInfo Net File containing primitive data for all nodes, edges and faces in the terrain. Primitives defining 3D buildings were obtained by digitizing "flat" building plans into three dimensions. Roads, previously existing only as centerlines, were also widened to their real-world width. VPF+ tables were then populated with this data.

Since the construction drawings of the buildings were readily available, we were able to create highly accurate interiors and exteriors of the buildings in a short period of time. We did this by using an on-screen digitizer and JPEG's of the construction drawings. The digitizer allowed us to capture the detailed geometry of the buildings along with additional information needed to build VPF+ Level 4 topology. This process required approximately two hours on the average to digitize a two-story building including all interior rooms, roof structure and exterior façade.

We maximized the user's experience within this synthetic environment by providing for movement and interaction consistent with the types of interactions expected of Marines during anticipated operations. For example, users can walk or fly across terrain, and they can enter buildings through doorways or climb in through open windows. The synthetic buildings conform to their real-world floor plans, allowing direct line of sight into and out of buildings through open doorways and windows. Once inside a building, users can enter doorways to walk through interior rooms or climb stairs to access different floors.

Figure 6 shows the user interface we developed for the prototype. The features, symbolically represented in the traditional manner on the digital map on the left, are reconstructed as an interactive 3D virtual world on the right. The 3D buildings have a real-world appearance, and the roads have real-world width. Other features such as streetlights and trees are placed according to their real-world position and are made to resemble their real-world counterparts.

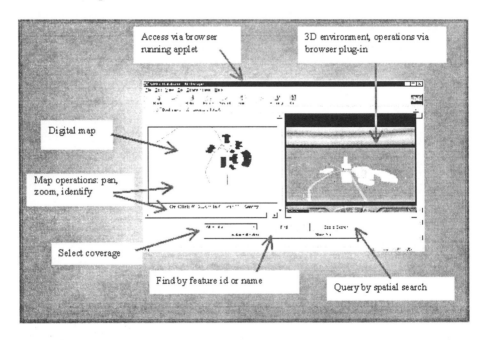

Figure 6. Prototype Mapping-3D Interface

Database querying is provided via s*patial search,* f*ind,* and i*dentify* functions. *Spatial search* allows the user to execute a simple 2D spatial query by defining a search distance and using the mouse to click on a point on the map. The search queries the database to identify features within the user-defined distance of the selected point. It then highlights the features it identifies on the map. The interface also triggers the database to produce the same features in full 3D. In contrast to *spatial search*, the user can apply the *find* function to locate a specific feature by name or ID number. The user input queries the database, and then it highlights the located feature on the map. The user then has the option of rendering only the identified feature in full 3D. The *identify* function is the visual interface counterpart to *find*. The user selects the *identify* radial button on the map display, then uses the mouse to click on one of the features. The system queries the database for the identification of the selected feature, then it highlights the feature and shows its name and identification on the map. As with the find function, the user has the option of rendering solely the identified feature in full 3D by pressing the Show 3D button.

Figures 7 through 9 show views of some of the buildings, roads, and point features in the prototyped world. The system intentionally renders doorways and windows as open spaces because the environment is intended for field operations requiring rapid entry and exit of buildings. The light-blue interior walls visible in Figures 7 and 9 appear in a contrasting color to easily distinguish them from the building's boundary walls. Each of these views is accessible by navigating through the 3D SE within the browser interface shown in Figure 6.

Figure 7. From Left, View of Church, Bank and Embassy Buildings at the Camp LeJeune MOUT Facility

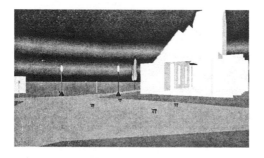

Figure 8. View Across the Townsquare at the Camp LeJeune MOUT Facility

Figure 9. View of Bank and Embassy Building from the Townsquare at the Camp LeJeune
MOUT Facility

4.   NRL'S GIDB

NRL developed the GIDB through a project funded by the Defense
Modeling and Simulation Office (DMSO) and the National Imagery and
Mapping Agency (NIMA) to produce a prototype object-oriented (OO)
database using the Digital Nautical Chart (DNC), one of NIMA's VPF
products. VPF represents geographic features, along with their spatial and
non-spatial attributes, through the use of relational tables. The GIDB was
designed as object-oriented (OO). This OO design provided a means of
addressing some of the issues that that accompany traditional VPF:
topological support among coverages, non-duplication of features among
coverages, improved data update, and increased access speed.

The GIDB has grown to support multiple VPF products (such as NIMA's
Urban Vector Map database), raster imagery, shape file format, video clips,
audio clips, temporal data and industry standards such as TIFF, GIF, and
JPEG. GIDB users interested in a given area of interest can obtain, over the
Web, a digital map supplemented with such diverse data.

The underlying motivation for having an Internet-based Java client
access the OO database is to improve access to NIMA data. Currently, users
of NIMA data must first obtain the data on CD-ROM or other storage media
and then must also have resident on their own computer systems software to
view the data. However, given NIMA's role as the primary geographic data
distributor for the Department of Defense, it is clear that electronic
dissemination and remote updating of NIMA's digital products is highly
desirable. The GIDB allows a user with a Java-enabled web browser, such
as Netscape, to access the database over the Internet and display mapping

data available for a given area of interest. Remote data update by privileged users is also possible.

Other features provided by the GIDB include:
- Spatial query - topologic, geometric and attribute-constrained.
- Network access with optimized performance by the server responding only to the specified request from the user.
- Local dynamic updating and modification at the feature or object level.
- Real-time updates from the data provider, such as NIMA.
- Export to VPF relational format.

The user interface into the GIDB is shown in Figure 10. It consists of a Java applet running inside a Netscape Web browser. The user can select from a list of pre-defined areas of interest or choose an area of interest by moving the red box over the world map, as shown in Figure 10. The interface allows the user to chose from databases, libraries and coverages for a given region, to more fully refine the area of interest, to query the database and to merge data from different libraries and databases. The result of selecting a 16 by 20 kilometer region surrounding the U.S. Corps of Engineers Field Research Facility at Duck, North Carolina shown in Figure 11. The interface also provides a "live" vector-based map. That is, after the map showing the features for a given area of interest is displayed the user can change the color of feature classes to make them more easily distinguishable and features can be directly queried for attributes without further interaction with the database. The interface also allows the user to add additional features, even from different databases, to the currently displayed map.

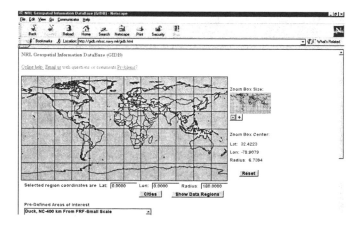

Figure 10. The GIDB User Interface

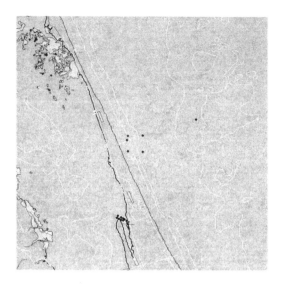

Figure 11. Sample GIDB Mapping Display

The U.S. Marine Corps has used the GIDB in two operations: Urban Warrior in 1999 and Millennium Dragon in 2000. In addition, the U.S. Navy is evaluating the GIDB for use on-board its ships. The GIDB's ability to integrate spatial and temporal data was also demonstrated in NIMA's Characterization of the Dynamic Littoral Zone project in 1999.

5.   CONCLUSION

Our prototype demonstrated the effectiveness of supplementing traditional digital mapping output with a three-dimensional synthetic environment in a Web-based approach. The VPF+ design allowed for a smooth integration of the VPF+ 3D data with traditional VPF data into a common database. VRML proved to be a reasonable choice for viewing the 3D synthetic environment over the Web. Since VPF+ is an extension of NIMA's traditional VPF specification, incorporation of VPF+ into DMAP's GIDB should proceed relatively smoothly. Integration of our 3D work with the GIDB will allow users access to digital maps supplemented, when 3D data is available, with realistic, interactive 3D worlds via an Internet connection and a Web browser. Additionally, applications requiring 3D topological information should also benefit from VPF+ 3D non-manifold topology.

6. ACKNOWLEDGMENTS

The authors thank the National Imagery and Mapping Agency and the U.S. Marine Corps Warfighting Lab for their sponsorship of this research.

Abdelguerfi, M., *et al.* (1998). *VPF+: A Vector Product Format Extension Suitable for Three-Dimensional Modeling and Simulation,* tech. report NRL/FR/7441-98-9683, Naval Research Laboratory, Stennis Space Center, Missssippi.

GIDB. More information on the GIDB is available at dmap.nrlssc.navy.mil/dmap.

U.S. Army Simulation, Training (1998). and Instrumentation Command, Orlando, Florida, *Synthetic Environment Data Representation and Interchange Specification Overview, Volume 2 of the SEDRIS Documentation Set*, 12350 Research Parkway, Orlando, FL.

Department of Defense, *Interface Standard for Vector Product Format* (1996), MIL-STD 2407.

Chapter 4

Automated Reconstruction Of 3D City Models

Claus Brenner and Norbert Haala
Insitute for Photogrammetry, Stuttgart University

Key words: City models, building reconstruction, virtual reality.

Abstract: Three-dimensional city models are of growing importance. The increasing practical demand is accompanied by strong research efforts targeting at the automation of acquisition processes. This chapter gives an overview of data sources, measurement techniques and automation approaches.

1. INTRODUCTION

In general, the notion of a 3D city model is used for a representation of relevant objects in populated areas, including man-made objects and terrain. Nowadays, it is often understood that this representation is given in digital form, sometimes indicated by the term "virtual model". Whereas the terrain is usually described by a regular grid of 3D points, the so-called digital terrain model (DTM), the objects on top of it require a more elaborate representation. Relevant objects are usually man-made structures such as buildings, streets and bridges, but also urban vegetation like trees and bushes. There are many aspects concerning the representation of those objects, the most important being usually *geometric shape*. Besides that, for visualization, information about the object's *surface texture* is of interest. Finally, attributes like land use or surface coverage of the terrain surface as well as object features like usage, year of construction and owner are sometimes required.

There are numerous possible applications for 3D city models, including architecture and town planning, virtual trip planning and tourism information systems, car and personal navigation systems and simulations for microclimate, air pollution, and propagation of noise or electromagnetic waves. The latter is especially important for planning the locations of telecommunication antennas, which is becoming increasingly difficult due to the shrinking size of micro-cellular networks. Of all the applications mentioned, this is probably the most pressing, and due to the huge telecommunications market, also the one which could finance major developments in the near future. On the other hand, it seems that personal digital assistants (PDAs), which are able to provide navigation and three-dimensional as well as tourist and commercial information, will still take some time to develop. However, considering current trends regarding the merge of PDAs, navigation systems and mobile phones into a single device, this seems to be a high volume future mass market.

There are still several technical problems which have yet to be solved for a convenient and widespread use of three-dimensional information, mainly concerning data handling, management and access. However, development will benefit from general improvements in consumer electronics, such as computing power, rendering speed, transmission bandwidth and miniaturization. Thus, most researchers today agree that the major bottleneck is the timely, effective and economical *acquisition* and *update* of huge amounts of three-dimensional data (Danahy 99). In consequence, considerable research efforts have been devoted to automatic or semi-automatic acquisition techniques.

2.   DATA ACQUISITION

1.   Data Sources

Possible data sources for the reconstruction of 3D city models can be subdivided into the two classes of remote and terrestrial. *Remotely sensed data* includes satellite and aerial images (panchromatic and multispectral), digital surface models (DSM) from airborne laser scanning using airplanes or helicopters, and interferometric synthetic aperture radar (InSAR) using satellites or airplanes. Satellite and aerial images can be used to derive a number of products: DSMs, DTMs and orthorectified images can be obtained by automatic image matching, co-ordinates of single points by standard photogrammetric point measurement, and thematic maps by automatic image classification. *Terrestrial data* includes digital and analogue images, single point measurement by theodolites and total stations, and dense range data from terrestrial laser scanners. Derived products are range maps from automatic image matching and 3D point co-ordinates from close range photogrammetric measurement.

For technical as well as economical reasons, not all of those sources can be exploited:

- Although in 1999 the first commercially available images from the Ikonos-2 satellite marked the begining of a new era, the ground resolution of 1m is still considered too low for the purpose of city model reconstruction.

- Interferometric SAR has been an emerging technique for years, and the successful Shuttle Radar Topography Mission (SRTM) in 2000 has attracted much attention to this method. However, the specifications of the generated DSM (30m raster width, 16m accuracy in height, and 20m in position (Bamler 1999)) indicate that SRTM data cannot be used for city model reconstruction. The situation is different for aerial based SAR sensors, however, in general, occlusions due to the flat inclination angle make it difficult to exploit this technique in build-up areas. In a recent study, height deviations of several meters have been found for building heights ranging from 10 to 45 meters (Mercer et al. 1999).

- The generation of DSMs by automatic image matching is often problematic in densely built-up areas (see section 3).

- Terrestrial techniques like geodetic measurement or close range photogrammetry have the potential to measure objects with an accuracy in the range of centimeters or even millimeters. However, in practice, due to the field work that has to be done and practical restrictions concerning accessibility and visibility, it is our experience that a single person can reconstruct at most a few objects per day using these techniques. Thus, although the methods are useful for obtaining highly accurate and detailed models, their application to the reconstruction of entire cities seems not economically feasible.

- Instead of geodetic or photogrammetric measurement of single 3D points, terrestrial laser scanning can be used to obtain dense range maps. Thus, for example building façades can be scanned rather than measured manually. However, scanning results in huge amounts of data, which can reach very easily several million 3D points per building. For this reason, the approach cannot be used to reconstruct cities with many thousands of buildings. On the other hand, using the scans for reverse engineering is very promising. For example, dense range maps can be used to derive descriptions of façade surfaces in terms of simple geometric primitives such as doors, windows and balconies.

Besides the data sources mentioned above, there are sometimes 2D ground plans available from manually digitized maps or existing Geo-Information System (GIS) databases. This kind of information is very valuable, since it is usually the product of some human interpretation. Thus, it can be used to "inject" human knowledge into an otherwise non-interactive reconstruction process.

2.   Photogrammetric Data Collection

Photogrammetry has a long history as a tool for the efficient and accurate acquisition of information for topographic and thematic mapping applications. Traditionally, photogrammetric data collection is based on processing airborne or space-borne images. The main products are:
- DSMs and DTMs, i.e. geometric representations of the earth's surface with or without additional objects rising from the terrain like trees or buildings.
- Orthorectified images, i.e. image data which is mapped to an external ground co-ordinate system (the mapping frame) based on an orthogonal parallel projection of the image. The transformation of the perspective image into the parallel projection of the orthorectified image requires information about the terrain height, which is provided by a DSM.
- Topographic objects, which are detected and reconstructed based on the collected imagery.

Besides efficiency and accuracy, one of the advantages of photogrammetric techniques is the simultaneous availability of object geometry *and* surface texture. This is used for the photogrammetric production of additional products like 3D landscape models for the generation of 3D views, animations or simulations. These products have become increasingly important due to the ongoing change from 2D maps to 3D GIS.

The basic principle of photogrammetric data collection is the application of overlapping imagery for 3D co-ordinate measurement. If a point is depicted in at least two images (stereo principle) its corresponding 3D object co-ordinates can be determined. In order to measure 3D point co-ordinates based on overlapping images, information on position (three translations) and orientation (three rotations) of the camera—the so-called exterior orientation—at the time of exposure are required. In addition, the parameters of interior orientation have to be provided, which describe the position of the image plane with respect to the center of projection of the camera. Both exterior and interior orientation can be reconstructed based on the image data, if object co-ordinates are available for a number of points (so-called ground control points). If more than one image has to be oriented simultaneously, tie points, i.e. corresponding image points are additionally used for the reconstruction of the exterior orientation. For airborne imagery usually complete blocks of overlapping images are oriented by a so-called bundle block adjustment. These algorithms have become standard tools within digital photogrammetric workstations, which provide fully automatic software tools to solve this task. Meanwhile additional observations like GPS or inertial measurements are integrated to avoid or reduce the number of ground control points and to further improve the orientation process in terms of accuracy and reliability.

If the parameters of exterior and interior orientation are available, object and image co-ordinates are linked by the so-called co linearity equation, which mathematically describes the fact that a point in object space, the projective centre of the optics and the corresponding point in image space form one straight line. Applying this principle, the 3D coordinates of all points can be determined by a spatial intersection of straight lines if they are observed in at least two images. Thus, for geometric reconstruction of objects like buildings, geometric primitives like points, lines and regions, which are relevant to describe these objects have to be identified in the images. Based on these corresponding image primitives the object can then be reconstructed in the 3D world.

3.   Surface Reconstruction

Using photogrammetry, the generation of a dense grid of 3D points which describes surface geometry requires the measurement of many corresponding (so-called homologous) points. Since this is very time consuming, starting in the eighties, methods for automatic image matching using digital image processing were investigated. It turned out that indeed automatic matching is feasible, mainly due to the fact that an actual *interpretation* of image points is not necessary—it suffices to determine which points are homologous. Today, the fully automatic generation of DSMs from overlapping aerial images is a standard matching tool integrated into commercially available digital photogrammetric workstations.

There are two basic image matching principles which have evolved. *Intensity based matching* uses small windows around the actual points to be matched. If the match is good, all the corresponding greyvalues in the windows must be similar. Since the images are taken from different directions, the contents of the windows will be different. Thus, a geometric transform is used, which does the necessary image warp. Additionally, a radiometric transform accounts for different brightness and contrast. All geometric and radiometric parameters are estimated by an adjustment procedure where the greyvalues in the windows are used as observations. Intensity based matching is very accurate, with subpixel accuracy of up to 1/10 of a pixel. On the down side, the estimation has to be performed iteratively, which makes it time consuming. Moreover, very close initial values are needed for the point positions.

In contrast, *feature based matching* first extracts features in all (at least two) images independently, and assigns the *features* (not the greyvalues) in a second step. Point features are most widely used for DSM generation. Their extraction is done by so-called interest operators. Point assignment in the second step begins from an initial estimate about a mapping between the images. Using a robust estimation procedure, the mapping function and point assignments are iteratively changed until a stable solution is obtained. The mapping function between two images directly corresponds to a DSM surface in 3D space. In order to remove outliers and to bridge gaps where no interest points have been detected in the images, certain constraints are imposed on the reconstructed DSM surface, usually the minimization of surface curvature. Feature based matching is often considered to be accurate to 0.3-0.5 pixels and thus is inferior to intensity based matching in this respect. However, it is faster and needs less accurate initial approximation values to start from.

A very good treatment of both matching techniques has been written by W. Förstner (1993). A principal problem of all matching procedures is their tendency to introduce smoothing. In the case of intensity based matching, this is due to the fact that a window is matched rather than a single pixel. Feature based matching introduces smoothing by the constraints imposed on the DSM surface. Some researchers have tried to improve this situation, for example, by using adaptive matching masks (Berthod et al. 1995). However, there is no widely applicable solution up to now. In consequence, image matching often performs poor in the neighborhood of jump edges. Thus, the surface of urban areas is usually not represented faithfully, especially at building borders.

Due to those problems, airborne laser scanning (ALS) has won considerable recognition as an alternative method for DSM generation, especially if a very dense, reliable and accurate data collection is required (Baltsavias, 1999, Ackermann, 1999). ALS (see Figure 1) is based mostly on pulsed lasers operating in the near infrared, which give return signals after diffusion and reflection on the ground. The travel times of the laser pulses are recorded to nearly 10^{-10} s and converted to distances. Precise kinematic positioning of the platform by differential GPS and inertial attitude determination by inertial measurement provides the reference to an external co-ordinate system. Area covering collection is possible since the laser beam is deflected perpendicular to the direction of flight, which—in combination with the movement of the airborne platform—results in a strip-wise collection of laser measurements. Typical scanning mechanisms either use oscillating mirrors producing zizag-lines (bidirectional scans) or parallel lines (unidirectional scans).

Laser scanning systems furnish geometric results in terms of distance, position, attitude, and co-ordinates. For each laser shot, the spatial vector from the laser platform to the point of reflection is established, thus providing the XYZ co-ordinates of the footprint. The overall vertical system accuracy is usually in the order of one decimeter. Most systems presently operate at flying heights of up to about 1000 m above ground. The scan angle is in most cases smaller than ± 20°. Some laser scanning systems provide, in addition to range, information on the intensity of the recorded signal.

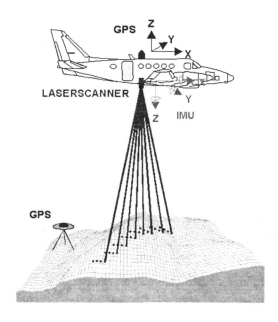

Figure 1. Principle of airborne laserscanning.

For data collection in urban areas, the high measurement rate of laser scanning is of particular importance. Present measuring rates lie between 2 kHz and 25 kHz. Accordingly, from 1000 m flying height, the sampling densities on the ground range from about 1 point per 20 m^2 up to 20 points per square meter. The actual sampling density depends on the system and on the balance between flying speed, pulse rate, scan angle, and flying height. Since parameters like flying speed and height can be reduced almost arbitrarily for helicopter based systems, very high point densities can be reached. For city models, a ground sampling density of one point per square meter has been a popular choice.

Due to vibrations and turbulences, the measured points do not form a perfect grid on the ground. Thus, usually the final DSM (evenly spaced points) is obtained by interpolation. An example of a DSM acquired by laser scanning is shown in Figure 2. In order to improve the 3D visualization of the data, an orthorectified image has been warped over the DSM surface. Although visualizations like the one in Figure 2 look already quite appealing, they consist simply of a connected mesh of colored 3D points. There are no object entities to which information could be attached, and the amount of data required to represent the model is huge. Also, building facades are represented poorly and all objects look like they have been "wrapped".

Figure 2. Laser data overlaid with aerial image for visualization.

Figure 3 shows DSMs from image matching (aerial images, scale 1:5000, normal angle lens) and airborne laser scanning. It can be seen that image matching captures the inner roof geometry sometimes pretty well, however huge errors may occur at building boundaries, which sometimes intrude into the building itself. The rightmost example shows that a high flat-roof building is missed by the image matching DSM but represented in the laser scan DSM (including the extra structure on top of the building).

Another advantage of laser scanning systems is their ability to differentiate between different responses of a beam reflection. When a beam hits the foliage of a tree, a certain percentage of the laser footprint is reflected directly by branches and leaves. The remaining part can penetrate the foliage and is reflected by the terrain surface. For this reason, the top of the tree corresponds to the first response and the terrain to the last response of the laser pulse (*Figure* 4). If the laser system is able to record multiple responses, this can be used for the detection of regions with trees.

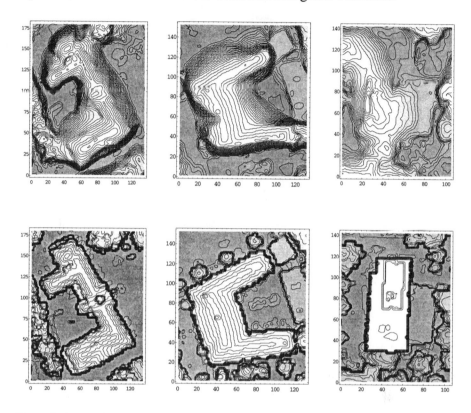

Figure 3. Comparison between image matching (above) and laser scanning (below) for three buildings. The plotted contour lines are in intervals of one meter.

Figure 4. Greyvalue representation of a DSM derived from first pulse (left) and last pulse (right) measurement.

3.   AUTOMATED RECONSTRUCTION

1.   The Role of Models

Models play an essential role in the recognition and reconstruction of objects. Even when objects are measured manually, models are present which guide the measurement process:
–   Some of them are implicit—for example it might be clear to an operator from the context of the project that a measurement of the roof is required, albeit single roof tiles are of no interest.
–   Some others may be dictated by the available data material, for example image or scan resolution.
–   Still others may be given explicitly, for example a minimum requirement on the size or height of objects to be included in the measurement.

The first point is also known as *generalization*. It is the process of deliberately leaving away information which is not important for a certain, given purpose. Automatic generalization is a non-trivial task, even in 2D, where the automatic derivation of maps of different scale has been an open problem for quite some time (Anders et al. 1997).

The second point in the above list is connected with the notion of *scale space*. For example, an operator would not be tempted to measure single roof tiles in 30cm ground resolution aerial images because they simply are not discernible. For a high resolution image, one can imagine performing a series of convolutions using low-pass filters of decreasing cut-off frequency (increasing blur). The instant where an object (like a roof tile) disappears is known as *scale space event* and the scale related to the corresponding filter frequency is the *scale of the object* (Witkin 1986).

Scale space and generalization are actually related issues. Every reconstruction of objects requires some generalization. Especially for automatic approaches, it is often essential to choose the image scale according to the desired generalization level.

In general, geometric models can be divided into *specific* and *generic*. Specific models consist of an exact and complete description, such as a CAD model. However, they can only be used in well-controlled environments, for example, in an industrial context. For buildings, generic models have to be used, which describe *object classes* rather than single objects. An example of a generic model is a *parametric model*, which defines the basic shape (e.g. cylinder), but leaves the geometric parameters open (length, radius).

Figure 5 shows some geometric models for buildings. Parametric models typically include flat-, ridge-, hip- and desk-roof type buildings. Using the Boolean operations of union, intersection and subtraction, combined parametric models can be built from them. Prismatic models are obtained by the vertical extrusion of a ground polygon. Polyhedral models describe all piecewise planar objects. Ruled models include cone- and cylindrical-shaped surfaces. Free-form models are the most general description, represented for example by NURBS surfaces.

Of these, prismatic models have been widely used, especially by telecommunications companies. The reason is that besides a ground polygon, only a single height value is needed for their description. However, especially in Europe, the percentage of buildings which are adequately described by prismatic models is relatively low. Many research systems have therefore used parametric, combined parametric and polyhedral models. Ruled and free-form models have not been used so far in automatic building reconstruction, mainly because their extraction is difficult and corresponding buildings are relatively rare.

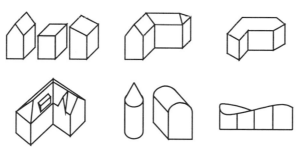

Figure 5. Geometric building models. From top to bottom: parametric, combined parametric, prismatic, polyhedral, ruled, free-form.

2. Building Reconstruction Systems

Reconstruction systems can be classified according to the following criteria:
- the data sources they use (section 2.1),
- the (geometric) building model they are based upon (section 1), and
- their operating principle: semi-automatic or fully automatic.

Historically, scientists have first tried to devise systems which fully automate the reconstruction process. The proceedings of the international workshop on *Automatic Extraction of Man-Made Objects from Aerial and Space Images* (Grün et al. 1995, 1997) give a good overview on the state of the art at that time. A popular choice regarding the data source have been aerial images, because they contain high detail, allow for precise measurement and are usually available in developed countries, eliminating the need to conduct a flight campaign especially for the purpose of building reconstruction.

However, these arguments do not apply in general. For example, aerial images which are available from public authorities in Germany are usually in the scale 1:15 000 to 1:18 000, often panchromatic, whereas color images in the scale 1:10 000 to 1:13 000 have been found useful for the purpose of *manual* building measurement (Wolf 1999). For automatic procedures, even larger scales of 1:5 000 have been used, also with unusual high overlap. Another problem is that images from public authorities are subject to fixed updating cycles, which are often in the range of several years. Thus, it is usually reasonable to invest a fraction of the total project cost into a dedicated image flight and be sure to have optimally suited, up-to-date raw material to start from.

It turned out that the high degree of detail in aerial images is not only a benefit but also a burden for any automatic reconstruction procedure. On the one hand, there is a high percentage of structures present in images which are not due to geometric properties, like different object materials, street markings, or shadows. On the other hand, geometric structures in the real world are sometimes not easily discernible in the images, due to noise, unfavorable lighting conditions or similar materials. Any automatic system thus must solve the very difficult task of selecting the "right" subset from an overwhelming set of features, and still be able to tolerate when important features are missing. This can only be done using a strong interpretation. In order to achieve that, the following techniques have been applied:

–   The use of a strong image segmentation. Instead of just extracting points *or* lines *or* regions, several primitive types *and their relations* are extracted. This has been named the extraction of *rich image attributes* (Henricsson 1995) or *polymorphic segmentation* (Fuchs 1998).
–   The integration of 3D information, for example by the use of a second aerial image, as early as possible in the extraction process (Baltsavias et al. 1995, Haala 1996, Fischer et al. 1998).
–   The inclusion of additional data sources like DSM (Haala 1994, Baltsavias et al. 1995, Ameri 2000) or color/ multispectral images (Henricsson et al. 1996, Mason et al. 1997). This has become known as the "data fusion" approach.

However, despite tremendous progress in this field, most researchers agree today that the fully automatic extraction of city models from images is not sufficiently stable and reliable yet (Grün et al. 1998), and "it can be doubted that automatic systems can achieve success rates comparable to human operators within the next few decades" (Förstner 1999). Consequently, many researchers have concentrated on the development of semi-automatic systems, which are meanwhile operational, some of them even being commercially available (Grün et al. 1998, Gülch et al. 1999, Brenner 1999).

It is sometimes useful to subdivide the task of "building reconstruction" or "building extraction" into the following subtasks:
- *detection*, which spots the possible locations where buildings might be,
- *structuring*, which defines the structure or *topology* of a building, for example in terms of a list of primitive objects and operations (constructive solid geometry, CSG) or in form of surfaces and their relations (boundary representation, BREP), and
- *geometric reconstruction*, which involves the exact determination of lengths and angles.

Typically, semi-automatic systems would leave the detection and structuring part to an operator whereas the precise measurement is carried out by the system.

3.   Segmentation of Digital Surface Models

The automatic interpretation of DSMs is often easier than the interpretation of (aerial) images. This is due to the fact that DSMs represent the surface *geometry* in explicit form, whereas images always leave some ambiguity which has to be resolved by matching features from different images. Especially due to the high density and quality in urban areas, DSMs from laser scanning are becoming increasingly popular as a means to aid scene interpretation. Therefore, in the following subsections, some typical applications and results are presented.

3.1   Detection of Buildings Using Morphology

Mathematical morphology is a well known method in binary image processing. The two operations of *erosion*

$$(I-s)(r,c) := \begin{cases} 1 & \text{if } \forall (i,j) \in s : I(r+i,c+j)=1 \\ 0 & \text{else} \end{cases}$$

and *dilation*

$$(I+s)(r,c) := \begin{cases} 1 & \text{if } \exists (i,j) \in s : I(r+i,c+j)=1 \\ 0 & \text{else} \end{cases}$$

are defined where $I(r,c) \in \{0,1\}$ is the binary image and s is the so-called *structure element*, a set of pixel co-ordinates, which usually form a connected set of certain shape, for example a rectangle or a disk. For greyvalue images I, this definition can be easily generalized by

$$(I-s)(r,c) := \min_{(i,j)\in s} \{I(r+i,c+j)\},$$

and

$$(I+s)(r,c) := \max_{(i,j)\in s}\{I(r+i,c+j)\}.$$

If rank filters are used instead of the minimum and maximum operators, a more robust behavior is obtained. The so called *opening* operation is defined as an erosion, followed by a dilation using the same structure element.

The application of the greyscale opening operator to a DSM, where the structure element is larger than the footprint of expected buildings, yields an approximation of the DTM. If this is subtracted from the original DSM, a *normalized DSM* is obtained, from which objects above ground can be obtained simply by thresholding (Figure 6).

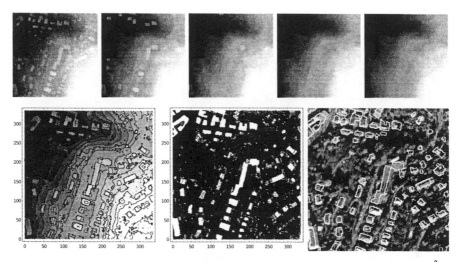

Figure 6. Top row: original DSM and openings with a rectangular mask of size 11×11m², 15×15m², 21×21m², 31×31m². Bottom row: contour plot of original DSM, normalized DSM, and orthorectified image with detected objects overlaid (threshold: 5 meters, filtered for a minimum footprint of at least 50 m²).

Several authors have used morphologic operators for the detection of buildings in DSM (e.g. Haala 1994, Weidner et al. 1995, Baltsavias et al. 1995, Ameri 2000). Although being conceptually very simple, it has the following disadvantages:

– the real building borders are usually quite different from the extension of the detected blob,

when moving from single detached buildings to a densely built-up area, determining a good size for the structure element *s* becomes increasingly difficult. Too small masks lead to defects inside large buildings, whereas too large masks lead to misdetections in undulating terrain, and

– buildings and vegetation cannot reliably be discriminated by this approach alone, especially when huge trees stand next to buildings.

Thus, building detection by morphology is mostly useful for finding an initial detection which can be refined, for example on the basis of aerial images.

3.2   Detection of Buildings by Classification

The analysis of multispectral imagery by standard classification algorithms is an alternative approach for the detection of cartographic objects in urban areas. One problem with the classification of multispectral data is the similar reflectance properties of trees and grass-covered areas. Frequently, the same holds true for the distinction of streets and buildings. However, trees and buildings can be discriminated easily from grass-covered areas or streets by the use of height data, since they are higher than their surrounding, whereas streets and green are at the terrain level. For this reason, multispectral images and DSM can be used as complementary data sources in a classification.

For example, Henricsson et al. (1996) use information from aerial color infrared images to distinguish elevation blobs of a DSM into the two classes of buildings and trees. Hug (1997) applies a scanning laser altimeter which is able to measure distance *and* surface reflectance. Since the laser operates in the near infrared, the resulting reflectance image can be used to discriminate between buildings and trees. Ford et al. (1997) use hyperspectral data with nominal 2 meter ground sample distance and over 200 spectral samples per pixel. It is captured by the airborne sensor system HYDICE (hyperspectral digital imagery collection experiment). Using traditional spectral classification techniques, a surface material map is generated which is refined by panchromatic image segmentation and fused with high resolution stereo disparity maps.

In the following, the combination of a multispectral color-infrared aerial image (CIR) and a normalized DSM from laser scanning is shown. The CIR image was scanned, resulting in three channels in the spectral bands of near infrared, red and green. In order to use the DSM, a co-registration is required, which is done by the generation of a color orthorectified image. As a result, a four channel image is obtained, from which a pixel-wise classification can be generated using a standard classification tool (see Figure 7).

Besides the detection of buildings, such a classification can also be used to find regions with trees, which can be important for simulations or for the automatic placement of "virtual trees" for visualizations. The right part of Figure 7 also suggests another possible application, namely the verification of existing 2D GIS databases. For example, in the upper left area of that image, it can be seen that the used map does not reflect the actual situation.

This information can be used to guide an operator based revision of GIS data.

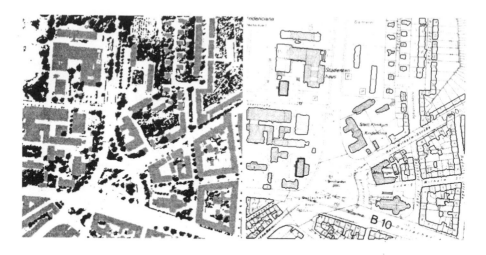

Figure 7. Classification result based on a CIR image and a DSM from laser scanning. Left: the four classes buildings, streets, trees and grass-covered. Right: comparison of an existing map and buildings found by classification (outlined in black).

3.3   Structuring by Curvature Based DSM Segmentation

If one thinks of the DSM as being given in the form of a regular, parameterized surface

$$x\colon R^2 \supset U \to R^3,$$

with normal vector of unit length

$$N(q) = \frac{x_u \times x_v}{\|x_u \times x_v\|}(q),$$

then, by standard differential geometry, the coefficients of the first and second fundamental form in local co-ordinates can be computed by

$$E = \langle x_u, x_u \rangle, \ \ F = \langle x_u, x_v \rangle, \ \ G = \langle x_v, x_v \rangle,$$

$$e = \langle N, x_{uu} \rangle, \ \ f = \langle N, x_{uv} \rangle, \ \ g = \langle N, x_{vv} \rangle,$$

where subscripts denote partial derivation and $\langle \cdot, \cdot \rangle$ stands for the scalar product. From that, the Gaussian (K) and mean (H) curvature can be derived by the formulas

$$K = \kappa_1 \cdot \kappa_2 = \frac{eg - f^2}{EG - F^2}$$

$$H = \frac{1}{2}(\kappa_1 + \kappa_2) = \frac{eG - 2fF + gE}{EG - F^2}$$

where κ_1, κ_2 denote the two principal curvatures. Considering only the signs of K and H, each of which can be negative, zero and positive, there are in total 8 different combinations (the case $H = 0$ *and* $K > 0$ is not possible). These can be classified into the three major cases of a convex, planar or concave surface.

In reality, since the DSM is given by discrete samples only, some care has to be taken, especially for higher order derivatives which tend to increase noise. Besides lowpass convolution masks, one can also use the estimation of local polynomial functions, as has been proposed by Besl (1988). Also, the sign function must be replaced by a modified version which treats small values as being zero.

Figure 8 shows an original DSM with 1m resolution, as a greyvalue image and its corresponding classifications into convex, concave and planar surface points. Although it can be seen that major structures of the roof are obtained, the results cannot be used directly. Specifically, since a relatively strong smoothing is required to suppress noise, curved regions of the same curvature class (convex or concave) sometimes become disconnected. Also, planar regions belonging to different roof surfaces are sometimes connected by thin pixel paths. For example, in the rightmost image of *Figure* , one can see that in the middle of the roof four regions are connected, although the corresponding roof surfaces have normal vectors in four substantially different directions.

Figure 8. From left to right: DSM of a building, DSM points classified as convex, concave and planar (classified points shown in black).

Thus, the classification of all DSM points into curvature classes can only be used as a first step in a processing chain. For example, Besl (1988) has proposed a scheme which first reduces (by morphology) and later expands (by region growing) the regions in order to obtain a final segmentation.

3.4   Structuring by Planar DSM Segmentation

For building extraction, a region based segmentation into *planar regions* is particularly useful. On the one hand, this is general enough to handle all polyhedral roof surfaces. On the other hand, segmentation into regions of higher order surfaces is often not sensible for DSMs of one meter ground resolution or lower.

When the points belonging to a region are known, the corresponding region equation can be obtained by parameter estimation. This can use either the distance measured perpendicular to the xy plane (difference in height), in which case the explicit formulation of the plane equation forms the basis for the observation equations

$$z_i + e_i = a \cdot x_i + b \cdot y_i + d$$

where i is running over all points and e_i is the error to be minimized. The parameters a, b and d are estimated from the given DSM points of the region using a linear (non-iterative) estimation. Of course, vertical planes cannot be handled.

Alternatively, the distance perpendicular to the estimated plane can be used, in which case a principal components analysis using the matrix of second central moments can be performed. From this, one obtains the plane normal vector from the eigenvector belonging to the smallest eigenvalue. A point on the plane is given by the center of mass of all points. Again, the plane parameters are obtained directly without iteration. In practice, the influence of outliers on the parameter estimation can be reduced by using robust estimation techniques like M-estimators (Huber, 1981) or the RANSAC method (Bolles et al. 1981).

The second—and more challenging—aspect of segmentation is how the points belonging to one region can be selected. Planar segmentation has been investigated by many authors, often in conjunction with depth maps in the close range domain. Techniques like region growing, split and merge, or clustering have been used. An experimental comparison of different approaches has been given by Hoover et al. (1996).

One especially popular choice has been segmentation by *region growing*. The idea here is to start from a small initial region, also known as *seed region*, which fulfils a certain predicate. Then, connected points are added to this region as long as the predicate is still true. When no more points can be added, the region is accepted and segmentation proceeds with the expansion of another seed region until there are no points left. In case of a planar segmentation, a suitable predicate usually is the distance from a best-fit plane, which is repeatedly estimated as the region grows. Possible seed regions can be ranked according to some local planarity criterion.

The main disadvantage of this method is its computational complexity, since points are added one by one and each addition has to be followed by a plane parameter estimation. A major improvement on this has been proposed by Jiang et al. (1992). His algorithm works in two steps, first grouping points into line segments, then line segments into regions.

Another disadvantage is that the result depends heavily on the order in which seed regions are selected. Ideally, one would like to extract large regions first. However, when a seed region is selected, its final expandability is not known. Rather, the selection is based on the heuristic that large planar regions will possibly also lead to one or more seed regions which are ranked high according to the local planarity criterion.

Figure 9 shows results of a region growing planar segmentation for two different DSMs with 1m resolution. The segmentation was only performed inside regions given by ground plans. It can be seen that in many cases, the segmentation corresponds pretty well to the actual roof structure. However, there are also roofs for which a very fragmented segmentation is obtained.

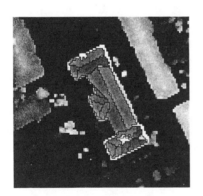

Figure 9. Results of a DSM segmentation into planar regions using region growing.

4. Ground Plans

Ground plans cannot only be used to delimit the extensions of buildings, but also to get some hints about the interior structure of roofs. In many highly developed countries, ground plans of buildings are available, although sometimes only in analogue form rather than in a digital database.

Most often, ground plans are described in form of closed polygons, consisting of vertices v_{ij} and edges p_i (Figure 10a). One can imagine a simple roof constructed on top of a given ground plan, where each roof surface Π_i emerges from one eaves edge P_i (Figure 10b). If all roof surfaces have the same slope, the projection onto the xy plane looks like in Figure 10c, where edge e_{ij} is the projection of the intersection of plane Π_i and Π_j, and vertex v_{ijk} is the projection of the intersection point of Π_i, Π_j and Π_k.

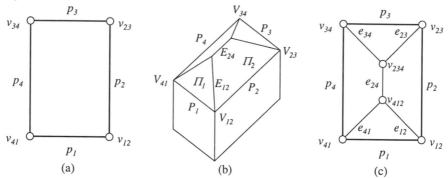

Figure 10. (a) Ground plan. (b) Simple roof constructed on top of this ground plan. (c) Edges and vertices projected down onto the xy plane.

From a ground plan, a projected roof structure like the one in Figure 10c can be obtained by construction of the so-called *straight skeleton*. This has been known for a long time but has received new attention recently (Aichholzer et al. 1995, Eppstein et al. 1999). Identical roof slopes are no requirement for the straight skeleton algorithm. Thus, the slope of each roof plane can be set independently, for example according to a value derived from a DSM. In particular, roof planes for which no hint in the DSM exists can also be set vertical. This approach has been presented in Haala et al. (1997).

It has to be noted that the straight skeleton algorithm in this simple form is only suited for roofs which fulfill the properties that
– all eaves have the same height and
– each eaves line P_i marks the beginning of one corresponding plane Π_i.
Even then, there might be more than one solution for a given ground plan and given roof slopes. All possible solutions can be found when the *constructive* straight skeleton algorithm is replaced by a *search procedure*. In this case, discrete relaxation and tree search with forward checking might be used to prevent a combinatorial explosion (Brenner 2000).

Another possibility for the integration of ground plans into building reconstruction is to subdivide complex plans into simple 2D primitives, reconstruct them independently in 3D, and reassemble the results in 3D. Figure 11a shows a U-shaped building and its subdivision into three rectangles. Note that it is also possible to introduce some generalization in this process by not requiring a full coverage of the original polygon. In Figure 11b, a set of possible 3D primitives based on a rectangular ground plan is shown, including flat, desk, saddleback and hip roofs. Using this fixed topology, the roof parameters like height and slope can be estimated from a fit to a DSM. For each rectangle, the 3D primitive with the smallest residual is selected. Finally, the complete building is assembled by putting together all 3D primitives using a CSG Boolean merge operation (Brenner 1999).

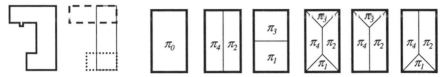

Figure 11. Left: subdivision of a ground plan into three 2D rectangular primitives. Note the small notch in the upper left part is not covered by any rectangle. Right: projections of 3D primitives for flat/desk, saddleback and hip roofs.

Subdividing ground plans into rectangles is an approach which works very well for a large percentage of buildings. In comparison to the straight skeleton, the class of *combined parametric* models is obtained, which allows different roof heights. For example, modeling industrial buildings which consist of several joined flat roofs of different height is straightforward. On the other hand, it is clear that non-rectangular ground plans containing round shapes or acute-angled corners cannot be subdivided reasonably well into rectangular primitives. If it is required to obtain a detailed model of these buildings as well, either a larger set of basic primitives is needed or the approach has to be combined with a more general method, possibly at the expense of a lower degree of automation.

4. TEXTURE MAPPING

For visualization, texture maps have to be associated with all visible object surfaces. Based on the reconstructed object geometry, the 3D surface patches can be directly mapped to the corresponding image sections if for all images the interior and exterior orientation of the camera at the time of exposure is available (see Figure 12). Figure 13 shows an example where the wire frames of reconstructed buildings are projected to an oriented aerial image.

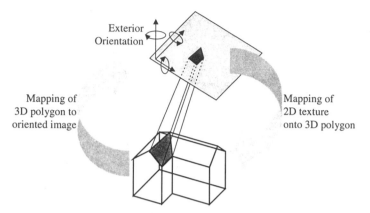

Figure 12. Texture mapping in the case of oriented images.

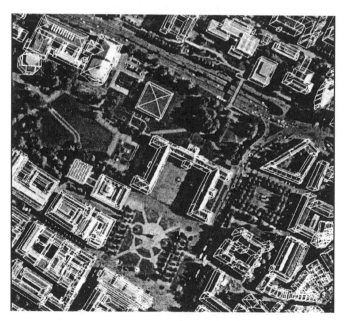

Figure 13. Wire frames of reconstructed buildings projected to an aerial image.

For terrestrial images, the case is usually different, although there are also systems which measure the orientation directly by an integrated sensor system based on GPS and an inertial measurement unit. For example, Bosse et al. (2000) use terrestrial images not only for texture mapping, but also for the geometric reconstruction of the environment. However, when the geometry is already available, a much simpler procedure can be used where terrestrial images are projectively warped and manually mapped to the reconstructed surfaces. Figure 14 and Figure 15 show examples from a visualization of a virtual model of the city of Heidelberg, Germany.

Figure 14. Visualization using texture mapping from an aerial image only.

Figure 15. Visualization combining texture mapping from terrestrial and aerial imagery.

5.   CONCLUSIONS AND OUTLOOK

In this chapter, we have given a brief overview about the generation of 3D city models. As we have pointed out, the *automation* of this process is a nontrivial task. Indeed, the degree of automation that can be reached in the partial steps of *detection*, *structuring* and *geometric reconstruction* is strongly dependent on the type of data sources which are used. As it is our opinion that DSMs often simplify reconstruction, we have treated some DSM processing algorithms in more detail.

Adding detailed textured faces to virtual city models usually implies a huge amount of manual work. Since often trees and vehicles are in front of buildings, they must be edited out, for example by the replication of other, non-occluded surface parts. Also, although the exterior orientation of each image might be known, small errors in the orientation itself or in the reconstruction of buildings may lead to a wrong mapping. Unfortunately, even very small errors—such as the mapping of a narrow stripe of blue sky to a façade—lead to strong disturbances in visual impression. Thus, it is not quite clear how the mapping of terrestrial images can be effectively automated.

When it comes to visualisations, it is often useful to distinguish between different classes of viewing positions. For example, Danahy (1999) identifies *overview strategic*, *close-range oblique* and *eye-level* visualisations. Depending on this type and on the desired level of perceived realism, the level of geometric and image detail has to be chosen. In this context, Lange (1999) presents a very interesting empirical study on the perceived realism of different natural and computer generated images, involving a set of 90 images rated by 75 test persons. It turned out that a terrain model draped with a high-resolution orthorectified image contributes most strongly to a high degree of perceived realism, followed by textured buildings for the eye-level scenes.

For the near future, we expect the following trends:
− The development of multi-sensor platforms such as laser scanning systems which also acquire co-registered color or multispectral images. Laser scanning companies have already begun to include cameras into their systems, and aerial cameras are currently on a transition from analogue to digital systems.
− The design of reconstruction systems which are able to deal with a wide variety of input data. In practice, it is important to be able to select the most appropriate methods depending on the availability of data for the particular project at hand.
− Systems using hybrid geometric models, making it effectively possible to profit from a fast reconstruction using predefined primitives while at the

same time not imposing restrictions on the geometry of reconstructed objects.

– Semiautomatic systems which integrate automatic modules but do not constrain the type of objects that can be modeled. It should always be possible for an operator to revert to a strictly manual measurement mode.

– The seamless integration of close range images, depth maps, aerial images and DSMs into one unified reconstruction system

IAPRS = International Archives of Photogrammetry and Remote Sensing

Ackermann, F. (1999). `Airborne laser scanning—present status and future expectations', *ISPRS Journal of Photogrammetry and Remote Sensing* **54**, 64-67.

Aichholzer, O., Aurenhammer, F., Alberts, D. & Gärtner, B. (1995). `A novel type of skeleton for polygons', *Journal of Universal Computer Science* **1** (12), 752-761.

Ameri, B. (2000). Automatic Recognition and 3D Reconstruction of Buildings through Computer Vision and Digital Photogrammetry, PhD thesis, Universität Stuttgart, Institut für Photogrammetrie.

Anders, K.-H. & Sester, M. (1997). Methods of data base interpretation—applied to model generalization from large to medium scale, *in* W. Förstner & L. Plümer, eds., `Proc. SMATI `97: Semantic Modelling for the Acquisition of Topographic Information from Images and Maps', Birkhäuser, pp. 89-103.

Baltsavias, E., Mason, S. & Stallmann, D. (1995). Use of DTMs/DSMs and orthoimages to support building extraction, *in* A. Grün, O. Kübler & P. Agouris, eds., `Automatic Extraction of Man-Made Objects from Aerial and Space Images', Birkhäuser, Basel, pp. 199-210.

Baltsavias, E. P. (1999). `Airborne laser scanning: existing systems and firms and other resources', *ISPRS Journal of Photogrammetry and Remote Sensing* **54**, 164-198.

Bamler, R. (1999). The SRTM mission: A world-wide 30m resolution DEM from SAR interferometry in 11 days, *in* D. Fritsch & R. Spiller, eds., `Photogrammetric Week 99', Wichmann Verlag, pp. 145-154.

Berthod, M., Gabet, L., Giraudon, G. & Lotti, J. (1995). High resolution stereo for the detection of buildings, *in* A. Grün, O. Kuebler & P. Agouris, eds., `Automatic Extraction of Man-Made Objects from Aerial and Space Images', Birkhäuser Verlag, Basel, Boston, Berlin, pp. 135-144.

Besl, P. J. (1988). *Surfaces in Range Image Understanding*, Springer series in perception engineering, Springer Verlag. Revised ed. of Ph.D. thesis, University of Michigan.

Bolles, R. C. & Fischler. M.A. (1981), A RANSAC-based approach to model fitting and its application to finding cylinders in range data, *in* `Proc. of 7th Int. Conf. on Artificial Intelligence, IJCAI '81', pp. 637-643.

Bosse, M., De Couto, D. and Teller, S. (2000). Eyes of Argus: Georeferenced Imagery in Urban Environments. *GPS World*, pp. 20-30.

Brenner, C. (1999). Interactive modelling tools for 3D building reconstruction, *in* D. Fritsch & R. Spiller, eds., `Photogrammetric Week 99', Wichmann Verlag, pp. 23-34.

Brenner, C. (2000). Towards fully automatic generation of city models, *in* `IAPRS, Vol. 33 Part 3, Amsterdam', pp. 85-92.

Danahy, J. (1999). Visualization data needs in urban environmental planning and design, *in* D. Fritsch & R. Spiller, eds., `Photogrammetric Week 99', Wichmann Verlag, pp. 351-365.

Eppstein, D. & Erickson, J. (1999). `Raising roofs, crashing cycles, and playing pool: Applications of a data structure for finding pairwise interactions', *Discrete & Computational Geometry* 22 , 569-592.

Fischer, A., Kolbe, T., Lang, F., Cremers, A., Förstner, W., Plümer, L. & Steinhage, V. (1998). `Extracting buildings from aerial images using hierarchical aggregation in 2D and 3D ', *Computer Vision and Image Understanding* **72** (2), 195-203.

Ford, S., Kalp, D., McGlone, C. & McKeown, D. (1997). Preliminary results on the analysis of HYDICE data for information fusion in cartographic feature extraction, *in* `SPIE Conference on Integrating Photogrammetric Techniques with Scene Analysis and Machine Vision III, Vol. 3072', Orlando, Florida, pp. 67-86.

Förstner, W. (1999). 3D-city models: Automatic and semiautomatic acquisition methods, *in* D. Fritsch & R. Spiller, eds., `Photogrammetric Week 99', Wichmann Verlag, pp. 291-303.

Fuchs, C. (1998). Extraktion polymorpher Bildstrukturen und ihre topologische und geometrische Gruppierung, PhD thesis, Rheinische Friedrich-Wilhelms-Universität zu Bonn, Institut für Photogrammetrie, DGK Reihe C, Nr. 502.

Grün, A. & Wang, X. (1998). CC-modeler: A topology generator for 3-D city models, *in* D. Fritsch, M. Englich & M. Sester, eds., `IAPRS, Vol. 32 Part 4, Stuttgart', pp. 188-196.

Grün, A., Baltsavias, E. & Henricsson, O., eds. (1997). *Automatic Extraction of Man-Made Objects from Aerial and Space Images (II)*, Birkhäuser, Basel.

Grün, A., Kübler, O. & Agouris, P., eds. (1995). *Automatic Extraction of Man-Made Objects from Aerial and Space Images*, Birkhäuser, Basel.

Gülch, E., Müller, H. & Läbe, T. (1999). Integration of automatic processes into semi-automatic building extraction, *in* `IAPRS, Vol. 32 Part 3-2W5, München'.

Haala, N. (1994). Detection of buildings by fusion of range and image data, *in* `IAPRS, Vol. 31 Part 3, München'.

Haala, N. (1996). Gebäuderekonstruktion durch Kombination von Bild- und Höhendaten, PhD thesis, Universität Stuttgart, Institut für Photogrammetrie, Deutsche Geodätische Kommission, C 460.

Haala, N. & Brenner, C. (1997). Interpretation of urban surface models using 2D building information, *in* A. Grün, E. Baltsavias & O. Henricsson, eds., `Automatic Extraction of Man-Made Objects from Aerial and Space Images (II)', Birkhäuser, Basel, pp. 213-222.

Förstner, W. (1993). Image Matching, Chapter 16, *in* Haralick, R. M. & Shapiro, L. G., *Computer and Robot Vision, Vol. II*, Addison-Wesley.

Henricsson, O. (1995). Inferring homogeneous regions from rich image attributes, *in* A. Grün, O. Kübler & P. Agouris, eds., `Automatic Extraction of Man-Made Objects from Aerial and Space Images', Birkhäuser, Basel, pp. 13-22.

Henricsson, O. (1996). Analysis of Image Structures using Color Attributes and Similarity Relations, PhD thesis, Institut für Geodäsie und Photogrammetrie, ETH Zürich, Mitteilungen Nr. 59.

Hoover, A., Jean-Baptiste, G., Jiang, X. Y., Flynn, P. J., Bunke, H., Goldgof, D. B., Bowyer, K., Eggert, D. W., Fitzgibbon, A. & Fisher, R. B. (1996). `An experimental comparison of range image segmentation algorithms', IEEE Transactions on Pattern Analysis and Machine Intelligence 18 (7), 673-689.

Huber, P. J. (1981). *Robust Statistics* , John Wiley and Sons, New York.

Hug, C. (1997). Extracting artificial surface objects from airborne laser scanner data, *in* A. Grün, E. Baltsavias & O. Henricsson, eds., `Automatic Extraction of Man-Made Objects from Aerial and Space Images (II)', Birkhäuser, Basel, pp. 203-212.

Jiang, X. Y. & Bunke, H. (1992). Fast segmentation of range images into planar regions by scan line grouping, Technical Report IAM -92-006, Institute of Informatics and Applied Mathematics, University of Berne, Switzerland.

Lange, E. (1999). The degree of realism of GIS-based virtual landscapes: Implications for spatial planning, *in* D. Fritsch & R. Spiller, eds., `Photogrammetric Week 99', Wichmann Verlag, pp. 367-374.

Mason, S. & Baltsavias, E. (1997., Image-based reconstruction of informal settlements, *in* A. Grün, E. Baltsavias & O. Henricsson, eds., `Automatic Extraction of Man-Made Objects from Aerial and Space Images (II)', Birkhäusei, Basel, pp. 97-108.

Mercer, J. B. & Schnick, S. (1999). Comparison of DEMs from STAR-3i interferometric SAR and scanning laser, *in* `Proc. ISPRS Comm. III Workshop, La Jolla, CA, November 9-11'.

Weidner, U. & Förstner, W. (1995). `Towards automatic building extraction from high resolution digital elevation models', *ISPRS Journal of Photogrammetry and Remote Sensing* 50 (4), 38-49.

Witkin, A. (1986). Scale space filtering, *in* Pentland, ed., `From Pixels to Predicates', Norwood NJ: Ablex.

Wolf, M. (1999). Photogrammetric data capture and calculation for 3D city models, *in* D. Fritsch & R. Spiller, eds., `Photogrammetric Week 99', Wichmann Verlag, pp. 305-312.

Chapter 5

Adaptive Capture Of Existing Cityscapes Using Multiple Panoramic Images

Ines Ernst, Thomas Jung
German National Research Center for Information Technolgy, Research Institute for Computer Architecture and Software Technology

Key words: Image-based rendering, point matching, epipolar geometry, photo-realistic, texturing, texture map, perspective projection, affine mapping, lighting, reflectance properties, artificial light, natural light

Abstract: Generally, the capture of existing cityscapes is an extremely time-consuming task. Although depth can be reconstructed from multiple views the reconstruction of complex 3D geometric models requires a considerable amount of user interaction (e. g. for texture editing). On the other hand there are techniques that allow panoramic shots to be visualized interactively in photo-realistic quality (e.g. QuicktimeVR). This article discusses the reconstruction of different types of 3D geometric primitives and textures from multiple high-resolution panoramic images and their synthesis into an interactive 3D visualization environment.

1. INTRODUCTION / PHOTO-REALISTC VISUALIZATION

Computer graphics techniques can be used to generate visual impressions of buildings and cityscapes. Walking through virtual worlds requires interactive graphics systems. Some graphics computers fulfill theses requirements for about one decade. Nowadays, nearly every personal computer supports interactive 3D graphics.

Most interactive systems just support local lighting models. But only global lighting models consider inter-reflections and this is exactly what photo-realistic image generation needs. Specular inter-reflections can be generated by ray-tracing (Whitted, 1980). Diffuse inter-reflections can be generated by radiosity methods (Goral et al., 1984). Both methods require much more computational effort than local lighting models. If lighting does not change diffuse inter-reflection can be pre-computed so that walking through radiosity-rendered scenes in real time is possible.

To generate photo-realistic images by using global lighting models 3D geometric models with rich details are required. Modeling such 3D scenes is a laborious and difficult task and leads to very large data.

Today´s interactive 3D graphics systems support texture mapping. Details can be described by images that are mapped to 3D faces. A few texture mapped faces can replace detailed 3D surfaces. Texture maps can be computed by radiosity methods. While diffuse lighting does not change with viewing position specular inter-reflections are viewer-dependent and cannot be pre-computed for interactive rendering.

Since most of the light which reaches the viewer´s eye (e.g. while walking through a street) results from diffuse reflection the usage of photographic information promises a reduction of modeling effort and promises also an increase of visual quality for the visualization of cityscapes. There are two approaches to photo-based visualization: image-based rendering and textured 3D graphics.

1.1   Image-based Rendering

In image-based rendering approaches, a geometric scene is represented by a collection of images, only. When the viewing position changes a new image has to be generated from the original images.

Usually, the optical parameters of the camera are not completely known. Moreover, the relative camera positions are only known to some degree of accuracy. This situation is called image-based rendering with uncalibrated images. For generating new images the following steps have to be taken (Zhang, 1998):
-   Establish point correspondences between images
-   Estimate the epipolar geometry between images
-   Build a representation of the scene using matched points
-   Specify the desired position of the new image
-   Transfer the scene representation into the new image
-   Map textures from the original images to the new images.

There are some approaches to establishing point correspondences automatically (Bergen et al., 1992; Zhang et al., 1995) but most cases need manual interaction. The epipolar geometry between multiple images can be described by p-matrices (Luong et al., 1996). A method for estimating these matrices is given in (Laveau, 1996).

If full pixel correspondences are available scenes can be represented by the original images. If only a small amount of point correspondences is available (e. g. in the case of manual selection) the images can be divided into a set of polygons using the pixel coordinates of the matched points.

Generating a new image requires a specification of its p-matrix because there is no explicit 3D representation. Since there are 15 degrees of freedom, the task is very difficult. This limits the usefulness of uncalibrated images (Zhang, 1998). Transferring the scene by using the p-matrix involves a lot of practical problems including occluding problems. Occluding problems are caused by transferring different original pixels to the same pixel in the new image.

If the point of view for all captured images as well as for the new image are identical then generating the new image is relatively simple. Images which are related by a linear projective transformation are called homography. The QuicktimeVR multimedia system (Chen, 1995) is an example for such a situation. A QuicktimeVR panorama enables turning as well as zooming in and out which gives an impression of approaching and departing, respectively.

1.2 Textured 3D Graphics

If the scene representation consists merely of a set of images much redundant information is saved because the capture of the same object from different camera positions contains similar image regions. In textured 3D graphics approaches a scene consists of a consistent set of 3D primitives whose textures are generated from the original images.

For integrating all images the viewing transformations referring to the scene coordinate system have to be determined. Like in the image-based rendering approach the internal camera parameters have to be known to eliminate distortions from the images.

Also, pixel correspondences have to be identified. Using the camera transformations the 3D vertex coordinates for every pixel correspondence can be determined via triangulation (depth from stereo). The vertices have to be combined into a polygonal surface. This process usually requires manual interaction.

1.3   Capturing of Photographic Information

The first important step is to choose camera positions. While satellite or aerial views provide a good overlook over a city area, photographs which are taken from the ground can have details that can be occluded in aerial views. Apart from minor costs pictures taken from the ground have the advantage that the camera position and the viewing position when visualizing the virtual scene are similar.

1.3.1 Lighting Conditions

The natural lighting effects kept in the photos represent only one moment in time and only one viewing position. If environments with other lighting influences should be rendered (e. g. sunrise or artificial lights) highlights and shadows in the textures are disturbing.

A simple way to mitigate this problem is to take photos only at days with covered sky. The more complicated and calculation-intensive way is to extract lighting effects from the images. Thereafter, textures will just keep material properties which allow determining new lighting conditions before rendering.

Usual image processing algorithms cannot solve this problem. By manipulating special color ranges it is not really possible to eliminate original light reflections without destroying the color impression of the pictures.

There exist low-cost algorithms to extract specular highlights but with weaknesses in handling of many colors or of grayscale pictures (Schluns et al., 1995).

The general solution requires determining a reflectance distribution function for every surface in dependence on all possible light sources and viewing directions. If there are only a few photos some simplifications for lighting and reflectance models and grouping of areas with similar reflectance properties can be made (Yizhou, 1999).

Some computationally expensive solution approaches are suitable for an adequate number of photographs and known artificial lighting situations (Yizhou, 1999). These methods are not applicable to situations in which a real environment is captured under natural lighting conditions in only a few panoramic images at one time.

1.3.2 Projection

Most image-based rendering approaches use conventional photographs which are projected onto a plane. Using panoramic images promises some advantages because the whole environment from one point of view is reflected within this image.

The QuicktimeVR system contains a tool which allows to combine a set of photographs into a panoramic image. The photographs are taken using a tripot head which rotates in discrete steps. The process of combining the single images is called stitching.

An alternative way is to use a special lens which allows capturing a panoramic image with just one shot, e. g. with a fish eye lens. This method cannot be used with current digital cameras since the resulting resolution is too low

Panoramic shots with a high resolution of 18000 x 5000 pixel can be taken by using a digital panorama scanner (Sasta, 1999). The camera uses a rotating CCD-sensor and guarantees images without distortions within the horizontal. These images are a very good cylinder projection of the real world. Every photo (see, e.g. Figure 1) gives a good impression of the environment of the viewpoint under bypassing the time-consuming and error-sensitive stitching process. The high resolution facilitates a substantial zoom "into" the picture if necessary.

Figure 1. High resolution 360-degree panoramic images

One disadvantage of these pictures is both the relatively high effort for taking a photo (not a hand-held camera, a tripod has to be adjusted) and the high memory consumption of the pictures with, of course much redundancy. It implies that taking photos has to be well planned. Photos have only to be taken at essential viewpoints and not as usually in stereo photography two pictures at nearly identical viewpoints.

2.   VISUALIZATION

Benefitting from using photographic information requires tightly adjusted visualization and capturing algorithms. Like in the QuicktimeVR multimedia system one has to take advantage of the special features of navigation through virtual worlds, e.g. a user has to walk on the ground, its velocity can be restricted.

2.1   Distant Adapted Representations

To simplify the rendering process it is reasonable to use simple support objects. These objects have to be provided with textures. Scene details which are recorded in these textures must not get lost while viewing the scene.

The closer the object is, the more exact the approximation of the real 3D geometry has to be. When coming closer to an object the change in size of the object in the projected image has been in inverse proportion to the square of the distance. For far distanced objects, e.g. mountains on the horizon, the perceived proportions does not change if the observer is moving. Therefore, these objects are fit to be shown in a scene-global background panorama (without any defined distance).

Surfaces can be mapped on plane polygons if the deviations are relatively modest or the current observer place is rather similar to the recording place of the photo of which the texture is obtained. The error of the projection in x-direction which arises while mapping surfaces on plane polygons is proportional to deviation as well as to cosine of the angle between recording position and viewing position. Also, the error is in inverse proportion to the distance of the object. Since, in most cases the depth of relief exteriors is lower than the viewing distance, photos of such kind of exteriors can be used as textures.

Objects which are both too far away to get reached by the observer and changing their size by getting closer to them, e.g. large buildings, can possess a relatively low angle between recording position and viewing position.

This category of objects can be represented in scenery images (see, e.g. Figure 2 (a)) each of which has been assigned to a selected depth value. This category of objects will be called middle distant objects in the following.

When dividing middle distant objects from background objects texture elements (texels) which contain object transitions are arising. These texels have to be assigned to the textures of both objects with complementary transparency values.

Foreground located objects (see, e.g. Figure 2 (b)) which can be observed from all sides have to be modeled as textured 3D models. Frequently, these textures have to be captured from different shots.

2.2   VRML-based Implementation

The Virtual Reality Modeling Language (VRML) allows describing textured 3D objects and scenes. VRML97 (Hartman et al., 1996) is an open standard for supporting 3D graphics on the Internet. VRML files can be downloaded and visualized interactively by so-called VRML browsers.

VRML scenes running in a VRML browser can be combined with other applications via a special interface called External Authoring Interface (Marrin, 1997). This is why it is fit for visualizing photo-based scenes.

Background objects can be implemented in VRML by using "Background" nodes which do not translate or scale with respect to the viewer. Middle distant and foreground objects can be implemented by using "IndexedFaceSet" nodes which allow describing textured 3D faces.

VRML supports several concepts to change the representation of an object when approaching or departing (e.g. LOD nodes, ProximitySensor nodes) so that, e.g., a middle distant object can be substituted by some foreground objects when reaching a special place in the 3D scene.

Figure 2. Browsing VRML objects (a) Middle distant objects (b) Foreground objects

3.   CAPTURING

For capturing a scene using panoramic shots, the following steps have to be taken:
-    Take panoramic shots
-    Determine relative camera positions
-    Establish point correspondences between images

-    Build scene objects (background, middle distant, foreground objects)

The generation of panoramic images was discussed in section 1.3. One way to determine the relative camera positions is to use two horizontally adjusted tripods and to measure the distance between them. Then, the relative orientation between the two shots can be reconstructed easily if one tripod is captured in the image which is taken by using the other tripod.

If the distances between multiple camera positions are not known and if only one tripod is available the relative camera positions can be reconstructed from the image data. This will be discussed in section 3.4.

3.1   Establish Point Correspondences

An extremely complex task in generating 3D information from panoramic images is establishing the point correspondences between different images which is a requirement for the reconstruction of depth information (triangulation).

Figure 3. Automatic point matching for similar image regions

Either automatic algorithms for point matching work only on the basis of extracted edge and vertex information or additionally with extracted information of camera parameters. The latter kind of methods are more stable and error-tolerant. As shown in Figure 3 Zhang`s method (Zhang, 1998) works well for similar images regions. The more different the images are, the worse are the results from automatic matching (see Figure 4). Similar images imply low distances between the viewpoints which can produce bad angle conditions for triangulation. Panoramic shots can be captured from points of view with a relatively large distance. In this case, a human observer is able to regard the same objects in different shots. Therewith, the images are very different and automatic methods will mostly fail. Another problem is that we cannot find all interesting points because depending on image quality lighting conditions and camera viewpoint, the contrast at the edges is too low or some points are hidden by foreground objects. These problems show the limitations of fully automatic methods.

Figure 4. Automatic matching for different image regions

Our approach aims at using manual selections of point correspondences and as far as possible supporting users by using the known epipolar geometry. A selected point in one image and the two camera viewpoints define a plane in space. The second image point also resides on this epipolar plane. That means, the second point has to be found on (or, due to inaccuracies, right next to) the epipolar line (see Figure 5) which has been the cutting line of the second image cylinder with the epipolar plane. It decreases the dimension of the searching problem. The computer can suggest possible matching points (points on cross roads of epipolar line and detected edges).

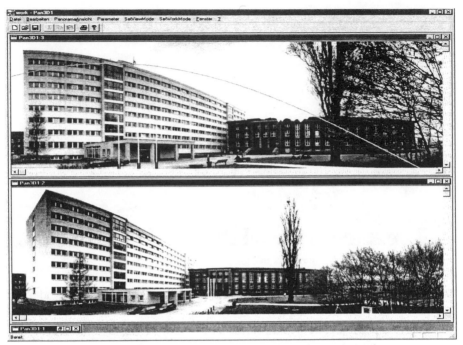

Figure 5. Epipolar line to support selecting point correspondences

3.2   Triangulation for Panoramic Images

To calculate depth information only from the images, every interesting point has to be seen in two or more pictures. In this case, depth information can be reconstructed via triangulation. Triangulation for panoramic images is shown in Figure 6.

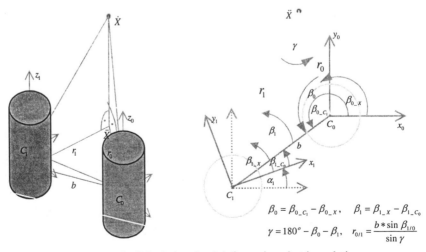

$$\beta_0 = \beta_{0\_c_1} - \beta_{0\_x}, \quad \beta_1 = \beta_{1\_x} - \beta_{1\_c_0}$$

$$\gamma = 180^o - \beta_0 - \beta_1, \quad r_{0/1} = \frac{b * \sin \beta_{1/0}}{\sin \gamma}$$

Figure 6 . Calculating depth information via triangulation

Panoramic shots generated by real cameras are distorted by the lenses. These distortions lead to errors in depth values. If the parameters of the lens are known, distortions can be reduced or eliminated. The panoramic scanner discussed in section 1.3.2 causes no distortion in the horizontal so that only vertical distortions have to be addressed.

Another source of errors is the inaccurate selection of pixels. The point selection has very carefully to be done with high image resolution to achieve sufficient accuracy of the coordinates. Badly conditioned problems (e. g. the camera positions and the selected point lie nearly on one line) let very long and thin triangles arise. The numerical errors can be so serious that they are unacceptable.

3.3 Building Objects

Single points have to be combined to faces. This can be done implicitly while users select points (see Figure 7). In this case, image regions which do not build a face in 3D can be fit together. This can be reasonable, e.g. for building middle distant objects. If only parts of walls or fronts have to be reconstructed edge detection algorithms can support building polygons. In every case, the faces should lie in a plane to avoid problems in the following rendering steps.

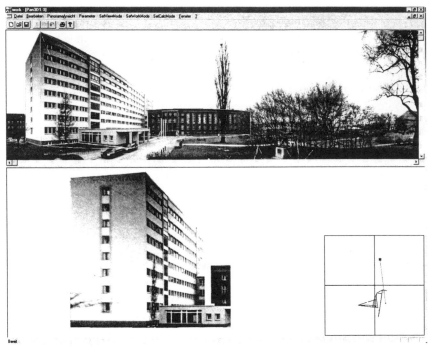

Figure 7. Combining vertices to faces, below the 3d model

Textures and associated texture coordinates are needed for all polygons for the subsequent rendering process. After interactive specification of some texture parameters these textures can automatically be calculated. The marked areas from the photographic images are not directly suitable as textures because they show the world which has been projected onto a cylinder. For texture generation, these regions can be cut out and re-projected. Accordingly, the polygons are projected in parallel in any desired direction. Figure 8 shows the two-step projection from panoramic images to texture maps which are suitable for using with 3D rendering engines.

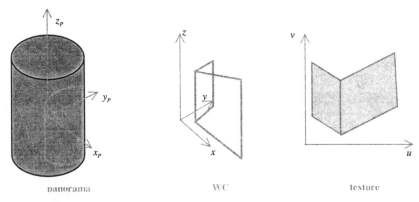

Figure 8. Transforming pixel coordinates from original panoramic image to texture map

Not every polygon needs its own texture map. Some polygons of a scene can be grouped. Of course, they must not hide each other in the chosen projection. Figure 9 shows a screen dump of the working system. The panoramic image can be seen on the head. The reconstructed orthogonal texture can be seen at the bottom.

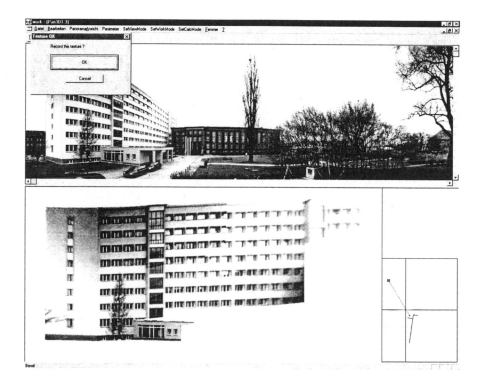

Figure 9. Texture maps contain parallel projected textures

3.4 Finding Camera Positions

Triangulation requires the distance between two different camera positions. If it is not the case we need a method for calculating this information automatically.

Usually, within two images, only parts of an object are visible. For reconstructing all sides of a building, we need some more panoramic images. The more camera positions are available, the more time is needed to measure the relative distances between any two camera positions. To prepare

calculations from these images, the panoramas have to be placed in a global
world coordinate system. In Figure 10 the images are uniquely characterized
by a viewpoint and a beginning angle.

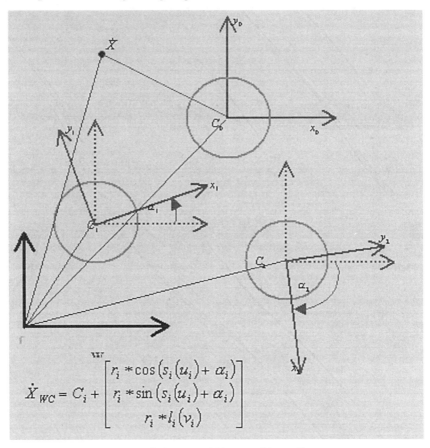

$$\dot{X}_{WC} = C_i + \begin{bmatrix} r_i * \cos\left(s_i\left(u_i\right) + \alpha_i\right) \\ r_i * \sin\left(s_i\left(u_i\right) + \alpha_i\right) \\ r_i * l_i\left(v_i\right) \end{bmatrix}$$

Figure10. Panoramic images within a world coordinate system

Under the assumption of ideal cylinder projections and strictly vertical
camera rotation axes, four corresponding point pairs are sufficient to
calculate the second camera point and the beginning angle of this image in
relation to the first one (see Figure 11). To eliminate errors it is better to
use more than four point pairs and to determine the solution of a minimum
problem. For sufficient and accurately marked point pairs (ten points should
be sufficient) and suggestive start values the multiplier method with linear
constraints proved reliable. The accuracy of the calculated camera point can
iteratively be improved with some more matching point pairs.

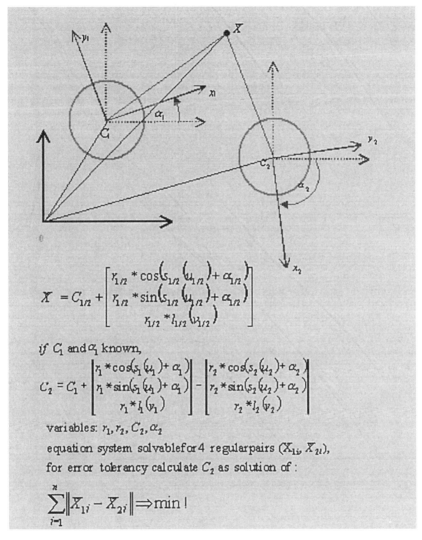

$$X = C_{1/2} + \begin{bmatrix} r_{1/2} * \cos\left(s_{1/2}\left(u_{1/2}\right) + \alpha_{1/2}\right) \\ r_{1/2} * \sin\left(s_{1/2}\left(u_{1/2}\right) + \alpha_{1/2}\right) \\ r_{1/2} * l_{1/2}\left(v_{1/2}\right) \end{bmatrix}$$

if C_1 *and* α_1 *known,*

$$C_2 = C_1 + \begin{bmatrix} r_1 * \cos\left(s_1\left(u_1\right) + \alpha_1\right) \\ r_1 * \sin\left(s_1\left(u_1\right) + \alpha_1\right) \\ r_1 * l_1\left(v_1\right) \end{bmatrix} - \begin{bmatrix} r_2 * \cos\left(s_2\left(u_2\right) + \alpha_2\right) \\ r_2 * \sin\left(s_2\left(u_2\right) + \alpha_2\right) \\ r_2 * l_2\left(v_2\right) \end{bmatrix}$$

variables: r_1, r_2, C_2, α_2

equation system solvable for 4 regular pairs (X_{1i}, X_{2i}),

for error tolerancy calculate C_2 as solution of :

$$\sum_{i=1}^{n} \left\| X_{1i} - X_{2i} \right\| \Rightarrow \min !$$

Figure 11. Calculation of unknown viewpoint from point correspondences for ideal cylinder projections

4.   CONCLUSION AND OUTLOOK

We presented a method for capturing and visualizing of cityscapes by using panoramic images, only. The user does not need ground plans of the area. Moreover, no further "on location" work is necessary. For carefully chosen camera points and panoramic images this tool is able to produce impressive models with moderate effort.

Now we are going to improve these algorithms for generating textures from two or more images, to develop algorithms for completing textures if they are not totally visible in one image and to find more robust and efficient methods for separating lighting and reflectance properties. Moreover, the usage of domain knowledge of existing buildings seems to be promising.

Whitted, T. (1980). An Improved Illumination Model for Shaded Display, Comm. ACM, pp. 342-349, Vol. 26, No 6.

Goral, C.M., Torrance, K.E., Greenberg, D.P., Battaile, B. (1984). Modeling the Interaction of Light Between Diffuse Surfaces, SIGGRAPH Proceedings, Computer Graphics, pp. 213-222.

Zhang, Z. (1998). Image-Based Geometrically-Correct Photorealistic Scene/object Modeling (IBPhM): A Review, Proceedings of Asian Conference on Computer Vision.

Bergen, J., Anandan, P., Hanna, K., Hingorani, R. (1992). Hierarchical model-based motion estimation, In Proc. 2nd European Conference on Computer Vision, G. Sandini, ed., Vol-588 of Lecture Notes in Computer Science, Santa Margherita Ligure, Italy, pp. 237-252, Springer-Verlag.

Zhang, Z., Deriche, R., Faugeras, O., Luong, Q.T. (1995). A robust technique for matching two uncalibrated images through the recovery of the unknown epipolar geometry, Artificial Intelligence Journal, vol. 78, pp. 87-119.

Luong, Q.T., Viéville, T. (1996). Canonical representations for the geometrics of multiple projective views", Computer Vision and Image Understanding, Vol. 64, pp. 193-229.

Laveau, S. (1996). Géométrie d'un système de N caméras. Théorie, estimation et applications. PhD thesis, École Polytechnique.

Chen, S. (1995). QuickTime VR – an image based approach to virtual environment navigation, SIGGRAPH Proceedings, Computer Graphics, pp. 29-38.

Schlüns, K., Teschner, M. (1995). Fast separation of reflection components and ist application in 3D shape recovery, Proc. IS&T/SID 3rd Color Imaging Conference, Scottsdale, Arizona, USA, pp. 48-51.

Yizhou Y., Debevec, P., Jitendra, M. and Hawkins, T. (1999). Inverse global illumination: recovering reflectance models of real scenes from photographs, SIGGRAPH Proceedings, Computer Graphics.

Sasta Metric System. (1999). http://www.innotech-ht.com.

Hartman, J., Wernecke, J. (1996). The VRML 2.0 Handbook: Building Moving Worlds on the Web, Addison-Wesley Developers Press.

Marrin, C. (1997). Proposal for a VRML 2.0 Informative Annex, External Authoring Interface Reference,
http://www.cosmosoftware.com/developer/movingworlds/spec/ExternalInterface.html.

Chapter 6

Urban Terrain Modeling For Augmented Reality Applications

Simon Julier, Yohan Baillot, Marco Lanzagorta, Lawrence Rosenblum and Dennis Brown
Baillot, Brown and Julier are with ITT AES/NRL. Rosenblum is with the Naval Research Laboratory, Washington D. C.. Lanzagorta is with Scientific Solutions

Key words: Augmented reality, virtual reality, urban modeling, terrain reconstruction, computer vision

Abstract: Augmented reality (AR) systems have arguably some of the most stringent requirements of any kind of three-dimensional synthetic graphic systems. AR systems register computer graphics (such as annotations, diagrams and models) directly with objects in the real-world. Most of the AR applications require the graphics to be precisely aligned with the environment. For example, if the AR system shows wire frame versions of actual buildings, we cannot afford to see them far apart from the position of the real buildings. To this end, an accurate tracking system and a detailed model of the environment are required. Constructing these models is an extremely challenging task as even a small error in the model (order of tens of centimeters or larger) can lead to significant errors, undermining the effectiveness of an AR system. Also, models of urban structures contain a very large number of different objects (buildings, doors and windows just to name a few). This chapter discusses the problem of developing a detailed synthetic model of an urban environment for a mobile augmented reality system. We review, describe and compare the effectiveness of a number of different modeling paradigms against traditional manual techniques. These techniques include photogrammetry methods (using automatic, semi-automatic and manual segmentation) and 3 dimensional scanning methods (such as aircraft-mounted LIDAR) and conventional manual techniques.

1. INTRODUCTION

Augmented Reality (AR) has the potential to literally revolutionize the way in which information is disseminated to mobile users. The basic principle of augmented reality is illustrated in Figure 1–a user wears a see-through head mounted display and the user's position and orientation is tracked. Using a model of the user's environment, computer graphics are generated; through the head-mounted display, they appear to be aligned directly with the objects in the user's environment. Experimental AR prototypes have been demonstrated in task domains ranging from aircraft manufacturing (Caudell, 1992; Caudell, 1994) to image-guided surgery (Fuchs, 1998), and from maintenance and repair (Feiner, 1993; Hoff, 1996) to building construction (Webster, 1996).

Recent developments in wearable computers have begun to make *mobile* augmented reality systems a reality (Feiner, 1997; Piekarski, 1999, Julier, 2000). Systems such as that shown in Figure 1 can now be constructed using commercially available hardware and software. With this freedom comes a new domain–outside of a laboratory and into the "real world"–and many new possible applications.

One of the most valuable applications of AR is its capacity to provide situation awareness to military personnel in urban environments. Urban environments are complicated, dynamic, and inherently three-dimensional, and military personnel need to receive data to ensure safe operation and coordination with other team members. AR can provide information such as virtual signposts (name labels that appear to be attached to the side of a building), routes (perhaps as a trail of breadcrumbs which need to be followed), or even information about various types of infrastructure (such as the location of power lines or water papers). This information can be presented in a hands-off manner; it can be integrated directly into the environment, and does not block the user's view of the "real world." An actual output from the mobile AR system of Figure 1 is shown in Figure 2. This image shows how various types of computer graphics (including the outline of buildings and windows) can be precisely registered against objects in the real environment.

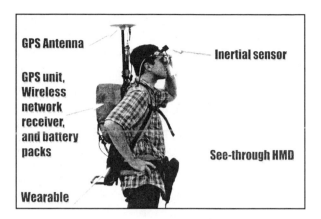

Figure 1. The hardware of the wearable augmented reality system which has been developed at the Naval Research Laboratory. The large size of the system is the result of the fact that it is developed from COTS hardware using non-modular components.

Figure 2. Actual output captured from the headmounted display of the hardware system shown in *Figure 1*.

However, an AR system is only effective if the computer graphics it generates are aligned with the objects in the environment. If the graphics are incorrectly aligned, the result can be a system that is annoying or possibly even misleading. There are several factors that contribute to the accuracy of the registration. These include:

- *Accuracy of the tracking system.* How well is the user's position and orientation known?
- *Accuracy of the calibration of the head mounted display.* How well is the mapping from the 2D graphics display to the view of the user's eye known?
- *Accuracy of the underlying models.* How well is the underlying environment known?

The first two issues have been extensively examined upon and reported in the literature. Azuma (Azuma, 1994), for example, studied the effect of tracking errors (including prediction lag) when a user looks at a scene whose properties are extremely well known. Holloway (Holloway, 1995) developed detailed error models that examined how the unknown optical characteristics of the display affected registration errors. These studies have shown that tracking errors are much more significant than calibration errors and, for most applications, calibration errors (apart from the static offset of how a user puts the display on their head) can be ignored.

However, the third issue–model acquisition–has received relatively little attention in the mobile AR literature. This is despite the fact that the importance of model accuracy is well recognized for AR systems. Indeed, it could be argued that AR systems apply some of the most stringent requirements of any kind of three-dimensional synthetic graphic systems. The reason is that unlike virtual or visualized display systems, where a user looks at a purely synthetic environment, an AR system locates the graphics directly with the real world. Even though a model might be qualitatively correct, quantitative[1] modeling errors are readily apparent. However, outside the computer vision community, it appears that little research has been done into the third problem of model acquisition for mobile AR. The prevailing assumptions appear to be that either the system is working in an environment where accurate models can be constructed (for example, in a laboratory or an operating theatre) or the modeling errors are secondary to the other types of errors that were listed above.

This chapter discusses the problem of developing a detailed synthetic model of an urban environment for a mobile augmented reality system. We review, describe, and compare the effectiveness of a number of different modeling paradigms against traditional manual techniques. The structure of this chapter is as follows. Section 2 describes the role and function of a mobile AR system in more detail and presents an analysis of the model

---

[1] By qualitatively we mean that the model, when viewed on its own, *appears* to be correct. For example, the model might contain the correct number of buildings that lie in the correct relationship with one another. However, the absolute errors in the locations of size and locations of the buildings might be many tens of meters.

requirements that provide a lower bound on the required model accuracy. In Section 3 we survey a number of different modeling techniques and assess their advantages and disadvantages in a typical urban scenario. A summary and conclusions are given in Section 4.

2.   MODELING REQUIREMENTS FOR A MOBILE AUGMENTED REALITY SYSTEM

The requirements of a model depend on the purpose to which that model will be used. In this section we identify a set of requirements that will be used to assess the appropriateness of different modeling approaches.

Our specific application is the Battlefield Augmented Reality System (BARS), a visualization tool which can be used to provide situation awareness to Marines operating in urban environments. BARS is motivated by the fact that with the proliferation of urbanization throughout the world, it is expected that many future military operations (such as peace keeping or hostage rescue) will occur in urban environments (CFMOUT, 1997). These environments present many challenges. First, urban environments are extremely complicated and inherently three-dimensional. Above street level, the infrastructure of buildings may serve many different purposes (such as hospitals or communication stations) and can harbor many types of risks (such as snipers or instability due to structural damage). These features are often distributed and interleaved over several floors of a multi-floor building. Below street level, there may be a complex network of sewers, tunnels and utility systems. Cities can be confusing (especially if street signs are damaged or missing) and coordinating multiple team members can be difficult. To ensure the safety of both civilian and military personnel, it has long been argued that environmental information must be delivered to the individual user *in situ*. Some of the types of environmental information that must be shown include:

1. **Information local to the user.** Information which is localized and is a function of the user's current position and orientation. This type of information will be overlaid on relatively large-scale features in the environment. Examples include:
   - Building data (e.g., name of building, known function and floor plans).
   - Routing information (e.g., path that has to be followed to reach a particular destination).
   - Signpost information (e.g., translations of road signs).

2. **Highly localized information.** Unlike the local information described in
   the previous type, this type of information must be accurately registered
   to specific features in the environment.
   - Warnings (e.g., the alert that a particular window in a particular
     building contains a sniper).
   - Infrastructure and utility information, such as the location of power
     lines, service tunnels and water supplies, including 3D representations
     of otherwise hidden features that can be viewed as if seen with "X-ray
     vision".

These considerations introduce two complementary sets of requirements
for the urban environment model: what elements should be stored in the
model, and how accurately must the positions and sizes of these elements be
known?

The first question is answered by examining the types of information that
will be shown to the user. BARS must be capable of displaying both
"coarse" environmental features (such as the names and locations of
buildings) as well as "fine-grained" environmental features such as
individual windows or doors. This suggests that the model cannot be a
"polygon soup" of geometry and textures. Rather, the model should be
composed of a set of discrete, uniquely addressable objects[2]. Any model
building tool should be capable of providing data that is compatible with this
objective.

The answer to the second question is highly context and domain
dependent. The effect of modeling errors depends on both the types of
objects that the user looks at and the configuration of those objects with
respect to the user's position. To address these issues, we consider the
motivating scenario shown in *Figure 3*.

---

[2] We do not consider the related problem of how these models will be represented and what
data structures will be used to store them.

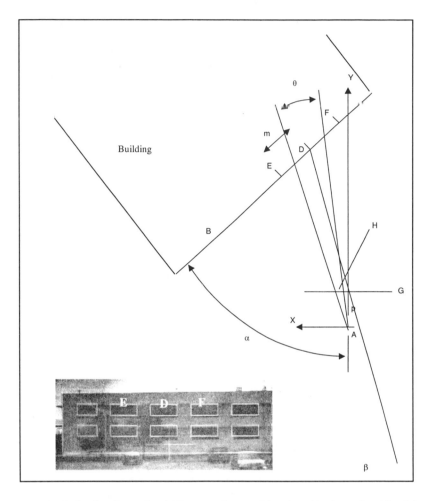

Figure 3. Motivating Scenario. A User stands at position A and looks at the side of the building B. The system attempts to correctly register the graphics on window D. Two similar windows, E and F, lie on either side of D. Other symbols are explained in the text

The AR system for the person (A) needs to be able to register graphics with the center of a window (D) on a wall of a building (B). The target window is surrounded by two other similar windows (centers at E and F respectively). The spacing between each window is uniform and is of length *m*. The user looks along the Y-axis. In general, the user does not look directly at the side of the building. Rather, the angle subtended between the user's viewing direction and the side of the building is α. The *augmentation error* is the difference between where an object appears on the head mounted display and where the computer rendered augmentation for that object appears. Because the optical characteristics of the head mounted display are assumed to be known, this error is equivalent to the angular error between the ray that points to the object and the ray that is formed by projecting the location of the graphics (drawn on the head-mounted display) out into the world.

Since the purpose of the system is to unambiguously show the user the correct window, we limit the augmentation error so that the computer generated augmentation of D lies less than half way between D and the adjacent features (E or F)[3]. Therefore, as illustrated in *Figure*, the computer-generated graphics should lie within the sector with interior angle θ.

The main factors influencing whether or not the augmentation is displayed correctly are the modeling and tracking errors. Modeling and tracking errors modify the size of θ as a function of the position and orientation of the building with respect to the user. Model errors are considered to be errors in position only because the models are generally constructed from the measurement of the location of their corners. Therefore, for a given modeling error the augmentation error will decrease as the distance between the user and the urban feature increases. Tracking errors affect both position and orientation. Tracking position errors can be treated to be the equivalent of modeling errors. However, tracker orientation errors lead to augmentation errors that are constant irrespective of the distance between the user and the urban feature. For this reason, estimating the orientation of a moving user is one of the most difficult challenges in mobile augmented reality (Azuma, 94).

Modeling errors have their greatest impact on the augmentation error when the urban feature is orthogonal to the user's point of view. Consider the case when the user looks directly at the face of the building ($\alpha = 90^0$). In this case, the horizontal error between between the actual position of the target feature (D) and the neighboring feature (E) is

$$m = e_{position} + e_{modeling} + 2 * Y_f * \tan (e_{orientation} / 2)$$

where $e_{position}$ is the tracker position error, $e_{modeling}$ is the model error in the position of D, Y_f is the distance between the face of the building and the user's current position and $e_{orientation}$ is the tracker orientation error.

The effects of this function are illustrated in Figure 4, which plots the maximum permissible modeling error for different viewing distances and tracker orientation errors. It is assumed that the windows are 2m apart and the errors in position are 0.1m. As an example, if the user looks at the

---

[3] The horizontal spacing between windows on the same floor is usually much less than the vertical spacing between windows on adjacent floors. Therefore, our analysis only considers the first case.

building at a distance of 35m with an angular error of 2 degrees, the maximum modeling error should be less than 0.5m.

To illustrate this function with a concrete example, we can consider the case of location of window on a building outdoors. We consider the center of the windows to be separated of 2 meters (m). An overly conservative estimate of the maximum position error of a kinematics-differential GPS is 0.1 m. State-of-the-art inertial tracking systems (gyroscope, accelerometers and compass) estimate orientation errors to less than 2 degrees. The graph in Figure 4 shows the maximum permissible modeling error for different combinations of viewing distance and orientation error. The analysis shows that, as the orientation angle and viewing distance increase, the maximum permissible error decreases. When the user is extremely close to the building the orientation error has very little effect and the model error can be of the same order of magnitude as the separation between the windows. As the distance increases, the effects of orientation errors become more extreme. With a tracking error of 3^0, and a viewing distance of more than 35m, exact registration is not possible even if a perfect urban model is used and other techniques (such as drawing bounding boxes that surround the urban features of interest) must be used. However, taking a nominal viewing distance of 25m and an orientation error of 3^0 implies that the maximum permissible modeling error is about 0.5m.

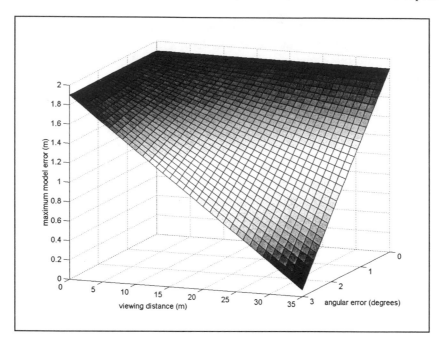

Figure 4. The maximum permissible error, $e_{modeling}$, for different combinations of viewing distance (Y_f) and orientation error $e_{orientation}$. For this figure, it is assumed that the separation between features, m=2 and the tracker position error $e_{position}$ =0.1.

In summary, this section has shown that the BARS mobile AR application requires the following:

• The model must be composed of building as well as "fine-grained" building features. These features include windows and doors. Each object must be identified individually – it is not sufficient to build a model that is a "polygon soup" of building shapes and textures.

• The maximum permissible error in estimating any feature must be less than 0.5m.

We now consider a number of different modeling approaches that are available.

3.   MODELING METHODS

1.   Surveying Methods

Probably the oldest (and simplest) approach to constructing a model is to use conventional surveying techniques. It includes equipment such as tape measures, theodolites, laser range finders, and kinematic GPS receivers. This type of approach is relevant because it can be used as the "ground truth" against which other methods can be compared. State-of-the-art surveying tools can give errors, when surveying a large site, on the order of centimeters.

However, manual methods have two obvious drawbacks. First, they do not scale well. Because the model must be constructed using many measurements, data acquisition and model building can take on the order of days. Second, certain types of building features (such as windows on a high story) are difficult to survey using these methods.

2.   Topological LIDAR

A common type of system uses LIght Detection And Ranging (LIDAR). This scanning method use the same principle as RADAR, and it can be thought of as a laser radar. The LIDAR instrument transmits light out to a target. The transmitted light interacts with and is changed by the target. Some of this light is reflected or scattered back to the instrument where it is analyzed. The change in the properties of the light enables some property of the target to be determined. The time for the light to travel out to the target and back to the LIDAR is used to determine the range of the target. LIDAR operates in the ultraviolet, visible, and infrared region of the electromagnetic spectrum. One of the most important practical advantages is that topographical LIDAR methods utilize an airborne ranging sensor to measure highly accurate distances to objects and surfaces. Distances from the airborne sensor are calculated through thousands of laser pulses within a scanned width beneath the aircraft. As a result, it is possible to acquire models of large environments extremely rapidly. Several commercial services, such as 3Di's EagleScan or TerraPoint (TerraPoint-00), provide commercial data sets of urban environments for municipal and government customers.

The use of LIDAR methods for topographical reconstruction can be traced back to NASA's application of LIDAR technology for oceanographic applications back in the 1970s. Although the US Geological Survey and the Jet Propulsion Laboratory experimented with these technologies during the

1980s, no successful low cost, high resolution results were obtained until the 1990s. Common LIDAR resolution ranges between 1 and 3 meters (X and Y) with a 1 meter horizontal accuracy, and delivering elevation accuracy (Z) of 30 centimeters or better. The ground coverage or 'swath' of the LIDAR sensor is a direct function of the altitude of the aircraft together with the scan angle (about 18 degrees to each side) of the laser itself. A general rule of thumb result is that the ground swath width to be one-half of the altitude height above ground level. So, multiple flight lines are required to cover wide areas.

LIDAR offer several advantages for topographical applications. First of all, it allows for the rapid generation of large scale Digital Terrain Models (DTM). Second, it is daylight and relatively weather independent. Third, it is extremely fast and precise in comparison to other topographic methods–historically, elevation data acquisition for the production of digital terrain data and DTMs was very costly and time consuming, and was usually done by acquiring and analyzing many stereo pairs of aerial photographs. Finally, LIDAR data can be fused directly with images to provide 3D textured models of an environment.

However, LIDAR methods are not sufficient, on their own, to fill the needs of Augmented Reality Systems. There are several difficulties with their use. First, the typical spatial errors recorded by a LIDAR model are not sufficient to meet the needs of mobile AR identified in the first section. Second, LIDAR does not, in itself, identify fine-grained building features. Rather, the best one can do is to use the LIDAR data and combine it with other data (such as images). However, as explained later, there can be significant difficulties unless the image data is extremely high quality. Finally, it is not clear that such approaches are capable of picking up crucial features such as the geometry in narrow alleyways. Together, these difficulties imply that LIDAR is not sufficient to meet the needs of mobile AR systems.

3.   Photogrammetric and Computer Vision-Based Techniques

A popular alternative to explicit range-based modeling algorithms are those that attempt to extract model parameters directly from photographs and video images. Given a sufficient number of pictures of an environment and sufficient camera calibration information (such as focal length and radial distortion), it is possible to construct a model of the scene at which a camera has been pointing (Maybank-92). Almost all such systems are designed to extract the geometry of buildings and to texture these to provide models that can be used for flythrough and other applications.

UMass's ASCENDER system (Jaynes-96), for example, provides a suite of software that allows the construction of textured models of an environment from aerial photographs. A calibrated camera is mounted to the bottom of an aircraft and a series of images are taken. Using template matching, the system uses an edge detector to determine the footprints of buildings, which are registered between multiple images. From this information, the geometric structure of the buildings can be determined. Textures are extracted in several steps. From those faces that are clearly visible, the texture is warped to offset the fact that it was taken from a non-oblique angle. For those faces that are obscured, the system has the capability to "fill in" and correct for the textures. Given information about the location of the sun, the system calculates the shadows cast from one building onto the surface of another one so that the color histogram of the shadowed region can be made to match that of the unshadowed region. Occluded textures can be extrapolated from visible building features.

Although these systems provide displays sufficient to meet the needs of many applications including cartography, land-use surveying, and urban planning, these models do not appear to be appropriate for our application. Many of these problems stem from the same limitations as airborne LIDAR sensors: the errors in the models can be fairly large and difficulties such as occlusion and the angle at which walls are viewed (near vertical) makes it difficult to recover the types of features which we need to include in the model.

Many of these difficulties can be overcome by using imagery that is collected directly from within the urban environment itself, for example, by a user walking through the environment. A number of software systems and packages, already marketed for computer graphics, are available for this purpose. One such system is Canoma, a commercial system that was inspired by the FAÇADE system (Debevec-96). Canoma uses a human operator to help identify correspondences between several pictures. The system is given a set of photographs that have been taken of the object to be modeled. The user identifies the same features (such as edges of buildings) between different pictures. The system then attempts to find a model that is consistent with the images that have been taken. However, we have encountered two difficulties with Canoma, both of which are illustrated in Figure 5, which shows a model constructed using the Canoma software. The first difficulty is that the software does not attempt to predict the accuracy of the model that it is constructing. As a result, it is only possible to assess the errors in the model by directly measuring them against ground truth. The second difficulty is that the texture is significantly distorted. Using this system, it is not possible to construct a model of the environment and subsequently use the texture data in any meaningful way.

A more sophisticated system for model reconstruction is PhotoModeler, developed by EOS Systems. PhotoModeler adopts broadly the same user interface principles as Canoma. The system uses a set of photographs taken from a calibrated (or approximately calibrated) camera. A user identifies the same features in multiple photographs and a model is constructed. Unlike Canoma, which only uses geometric primitives, PhotoModeler can be used to register point or line features. In Figure 6 we show a set of input images to PhotoModeler. These consist of the outline of the building as well as certain critical features such as windows or doors. The generated model is shown in Figure 7.

Wasilewski (Wasilewski-96) has developed a toolkit for urban terrain construction that combines elements of both aerial photogrammetry with the precise reconstruction from the PhotoModeler system. The model is constructed in several stages. First, aerial images are used to identify the footprints of buildings. Height is also entered (if it is already known) or is estimated from the shadows cast by the buildings. Finer-scale structures are reconstructed using PhotoModeler.

However, the greatest difficulty with manual systems such as those described here is the problem of scale. Because a manual operator must analyze each photograph and identify the correspondences between successive images, constructing a model can be an extremely difficult process. Therefore, a number of authors are attempting to develop systems that minimize the role that must be played by a user. These systems usually attempt to estimate structure (what a camera looks at) and motion (how the camera moves through the scene). Unlike the manual approaches described above, these systems attempt to track image primitives (or tokens) between multiple frames (Beardsley-95, Ayache-87, Zhang-92, Faugeras-98). Furthermore, these systems attempt to estimate the parameters of the camera directly as well, obviating the need for a calibrated camera. Although progress in this research seems extremely encouraging, most systems and results only consider the problem of developing a relatively small number of models (e.g., for a single building).

Figure 5. Model constructed using MetaCreation's Canoma software package. Note that although the broad geometric relationship between the buildings is correct, the textured building features (important for a mobile AR application) show significant distortion

Figure 6. Input images required to build the model shown below. In this (and similar manual systems) the user takes a series of photographs using a calibrated camera. The user then manually identifies common features between groups of photographs. In this case, the user identifies edges of the building as well as significant features (windows and a partially open door on the top floor of the main building).

Figure 7. Model of test building constructed using EOS System's PhotoModeler system. The user has to manually register the location of the individual features. The software assesses its accuracy using dimensionless units

Recently, MIT has embarked on the MIT City Scanning Project (Teller-98). The purpose of this project is to make a fully automated system for building an end-to-end system that "scans" an urban environment and constructs a 3D model that is suitable for use within a CAD package. A mobile robot is driven along a prearranged path. Every 10-15 meters the vehicle stops and, using a high resolution camera which is mounted on a pan or tilt head, the system records a mosaic of 47 or 71 images. These images are combined to form high resolution panoramic images at each location. The collection of images, known as a pose image dataset, is processed using a collection of algorithms to identify buildings and building structures. Although the scope and scalability of this algorithm is ideal for our application, there do not appear to be any detailed results published yet as to the actual accuracy achieved with the system. Columbia University is also developing a mobile robot that incorporates range and vision data in its urban model reconstruction efforts (Reed-99, Gueorguiev-00). Although this system does not appear to be as mature as the MIT system, it has the potential to automatically construct accurate urban models of sufficient accuracy, detail and resolution that they can be used with a mobile augmented reality system.

4. CONCLUSIONS

In this chapter we have considered the problem of constructing the model of an urban environment for mobile augmented reality applications. Unlike fly through, walk through, and other types of virtual reality applications, augmented reality applies two strict conditions. First, the models must be extremely accurate. A preliminary analysis suggests that errors cannot exceed 0.5m. Second, because the system must highlight individual building features, it is not sufficient to extract the geometry of the buildings and simply apply a texture to them.

We have considered a number of systems, both commercially available and currently under academic research, which aspire to construct urban models. However, although many of these systems yield models that are qualitatively correct, most do not meet our conditions identified earlier. Either the systems are not able to yield models of sufficient accuracy (for example, errors in LIDAR measurements are twice our acceptable levels) or the systems are not capable of identifying individual features.

Of the methods we have surveyed, we believe that two types of systems are likely to be most applicable. The first are the largely manual methods and, in particular, precision photogrammetric systems such as PhotoModeler. These systems are established products and have been available for many years. However, the problem with these systems is that they can be highly labor intensive and, as a result, constructing a model of a large-scale urban environment can be an extremely difficult prospect. Second, the fully autonomous systems currently under development appear extremely promising both in terms of the potential accuracy and detail of the models that they construct.

Ayache, N., and Lustman, F. (1987). Fast and Reliable Passive Trinocular Stereovision, Proceedings of the International Conference on Computer Vision.

Azuma, R., and Bishop, G. (1994). Improving Static and Dynamic Registration in an Optical See-Through HMD, Proceedings of SIGGRAPH 94, Orlando, Florida.

Beardsley, P., Torr, P., and Zisserman, A. (1995). 3D Model Acquisition from Extended Image Sequences, Oxford University Technical Report No. OUEL 2089/96.

Brooks, F. (1999). What's Real About Virtual Reality?, *Computer Graphics and Applications*, November/December 1999, pp. 16–27.

Caudell, T.P., and Mizell, D.W. (1992). Augmented Reality: An Application of Heads-Up Display Technology to Manual Manufacturing Processes, *Proceedings of 1992 IEEE Hawaii International Conference on Systems Sciences*, January.

Caudell, T.P. (1994). Introduction to Augmented Reality, *Proceedings of the Conference on Telemanipulator and Telepresence Technologies*, SPIE, Vol. 2351.

Concept Division, Marine Corps Combat Development Command "CMOUT". (1997). A Concept for Future Military Operations on Urbanized Terrain.

Debevec, P.E., Camillo J. T., and Malik, J. (1996). Modeling and Rendering Architecture from Photographs. In SIGGRAPH '96.

Faugeras, O., Rober, L., Laveau, S., Csurka, G., Zeller, C., Gauclin, C., and Zoghlami, I. (1997). 3-D Reconstruction of Urban Scenes from Image Sequences, *CVGIP-IU.*

Feiner, S., MacIntyre, B., Seligmann, D. (1993). Knowledge-based Augmented Reality, Communications of the ACM, Vol.37, No.6, pp. 52-62

Feiner, S., MacIntyre, B., Höllerer, T., and Webster, T. (1997). A Touring Machine: Prototyping 3D mobile augmented reality systems for exploring the urban environment, *Proceedings of the International Symposium on Wearable Computers,* Cambridge MA.

Fuchs, H., Livingston, M., Raskar, R., Colucci, D., Keller, K., State, A., Crawford, J., Rademacher, P., Drake, S., and Meyer, A. (1998). Augmented Reality Visualization for Laparoscopic Surgery, *Proceedings of the First International Conference on Medical Image Computing and Computer-Assisted Intervention (MICCAI '98).*

Gueorguiev, A., Allen, P., Gold, E., and Blaer, P. (2000). Design, Architecture, and Control of a Mobile Site Modeling Robot, IEEE Int. Conf. on Robotics and Automation, San Francisco.

Hoff, W.A., Lyon, T., and Nguyen, K. (1996). Computer Vision-Based Registration Techniques for Augmented Reality, *The Proceedings of Intelligent Robots and Control Systems XV, Intelligent Control Systems and Advanced Manufacturing,* SPIE, Vol. 2904, pp. 538-548.

Holloway, R. (1995). Registration Errors in Augmented Reality Systems, PhD dissertation, University of North Carolina at Chapel Hill. TR95-016.

Jaynes, C., Collins, R., Cheng, Y.Q., Wang, X.Q., Stolle, F., Schultz, F., Hanson, A., and Riseman, E. (1996). Automatic Construction of Three-Dimensional Models of Buildings, in ARPA IU RADIUS, Edited by: Yiannis Aloimonos.

Julier, S., Baillot, Y., Lanzagorta, M., Brown, D., and Rosenblum, L. (2000). BARS: Battlefield Augmented Reality System, Presented at the 2000 International Information Systems Technology Panel (IST) Symposium New Information Processing Techniques for Military Systems.

Maybank, S. and Faugeras, O. (1992). A Theory of Self-Calibration of a Moving Camera, International Journal of Computer Vision, 8(2):123-151.

Piekarski, W., Gunther, B., and Thomas, B. (1999). Integrating Virtual and Augmented Realities in an Outdoor Application, Proceedings of the Second International Workshop on Augmented Reality, pp. 45 – 54, October 20-21.

Reed, M., and Allen, P. (1999). 3-D Modeling from Range Imagery: An Incremental Method with a Planning Component, Image and Vision Computing, V. 17, pp. 99-111, 1999.

Teller, S. (1998). Automated Urban Model Acquisition: Project Rationale and Status, Proceedings of the 1998 Image Understanding Workshop, pp. 455-462.

TerraPoint (2000). 3D LIDAR: PRECISE BATTLE SPACE VISUALIZATION, http://www.transamerica.com/Business_Services/Real_Estate/TerraPoint/White_Paper/default.asp.

Wasilewski, T., Faust, N. and Ribarsky, W. (1996). Semi-Automated and Interactive Construction of 3D Urban Terrain Models.

Webster, A., Feiner, S., MacIntyre, B., Massie, W., and Krueger, T. (1996). Augmented reality applications in architectural construction", *Designing Digital Space: An Architect's Guide to Virtual Reality,* Ed. D. Bertol, Pub. John Wiley & Sons, pp. 193–200.

Zhang, Z., and Faugeras, O. (1992). 3D Dynamic Scene Analysis, Springer-Verlag.

Chapter 7

Development Of Tools For Construction Of Urban Databases And Their Efficient Visualization

Nickolas Fause, William Ribarsky
Center for GIS and Spatial Analysis Technologies,Graphics, Visualization, and Usability Center, Georgia Institute of Technolog

Key words: Shadows, Visualization, Photogrammetry, 3D.

Abstract: This work is focused on the rapid and easy development of 3 Dimensional Urban databases for use in real time visualization. Discussed is a semi-automated technique for the creation of 3 D models for urban structures. Interactive techniques for merger of both overhead and perspective (oblique) images are developed that allow easy association of building textures from oblique images with 3 D objects whose height is calculated on relative shadow length and/or number of story information from the perspective images. For detailed and unique structures, a commercial close range photogrammetry technique is interfaces. The tools are implemented in a Windows NT environment and directly export objects into the Georgia Tech developed GT-VGIS system which combines imagery from remote sensing, Geographic Information System (GIS) functionality, and real time scene visualization on a PC platform. Level of detail for 3D objects as well as for multiple resolutions of terrain are handled within the GT-VGIS system.

1. INTRODUCTION

Visualization of 3D urban environments including terrain, imagery and maps, buildings, roads and bridges, and other features is useful for city planning, reconnaissance, real estate development, emergency response, tourism, and other areas. Accurate geolocation and accurate relative scale of objects and features are important in these applications. Concurrent with these needs is an explosive growth of data at 1 M resolution or greater from precision aerial photography, high-resolution satellites, and extra high-resolution techniques such as LIDAR. Unfortunately until recently the process of extracting precision, geolocated features, objects, and terrain has been painstaking and by hand. This will not do for the amount of data available now.

Recent advances in building databases of objects such as buildings and other 3D features can be divided into two categories: automated and semi-automated methods. Automated methods include those that produce accurate flythroughs for a range of trajectories but without geolocation and those that produce accurately geolocated objects including geometry. In this paper we will discuss both types of methods but will focus on semi-automated methods

2.   DATA SOURCES

With the advent of unmanned air vehicles and all-weather imaging sensors it has become feasible to produce 3D terrain models on demand. To take full advantage of these new data sources, a terrain reconstruction system must be capable of rapidly and accurately generating new (or updating existing) digital terrain models (DTM) from images generated by a variety of sensors and viewing conditions. These sensors include electro-optical and radar.   The viewing conditions may include widely spaced sensors and oblique incidence angles.

Now high-resolution data sources that would support the urban 3D-database generation process are becoming much more available. There are now several satellites launched by private United States companies with 1 to 3 meter resolution and multispectral capability. Some of these systems have off-angle and stereo capability. Numerous foreign systems are also in the planning stages with equivalent resolution. Without using classified sources, it is possible to extract much of the information necessary to build 3D urban databases. The problem in building high resolution databases is not access to data, as it was in the past, it is how to efficiently process this massive amount of data with intelligent techniques to produce information to support modeling and simulation in urban environments.

Terrain elevation (Digital Terrain Elevation Data (DTED)) may be obtained from NIMA at standard Level 2 resolution (30 meters spacing and 5-10 meter elevation accuracy). If available, higher resolution in x, y, and z is also provided in a Level 2 format. High-resolution elevation data may also be extracted from stereo aerial photos or from the French SPOT satellite stereo imagery. Most of the 1 to 3 meter commercial systems have stereo capability also, but information must be provided about the camera model for each system for elevation extraction to take place. Commercial software products such as ERDAS Orthomax and Vision Softplotter have the capability for elevation extraction from stereo digital data sets.

Feature and cultural information can also be obtained from NIMA in the form of Level 1, Level 1C, and Level 2 Digital Feature Analysis Data (DFAD). Basic DFAD provides information as to the location of major terrain feature categories such as forest, water, open land, and urban, with some information as to manmade structures. DFAD Level 1C adds significant information about Lines of Communication (LOC). Level 2 provides considerably more detail about structures and facilities. This data source can provide information in urban areas similar to the road network, building footprint, and building height data used in the above urban prototype system. Detailed building height information could also be supplied by stereo exploitation of high-resolution image data sets.

3.   BACKGROUND WORK ON URBAN DATABASE CONSTRUCTION

With all these data sources, the question has become how to build extensive urban databases with appropriate detail in an automated or semi-automated fashion. For the purposes of this paper, we are not referring to urban databases composed of extremely detailed building models, such as those derived from building plans and typically constructed using CAD systems. Such models produce non-interactive visualizations. It may take minutes to hours to compute flythroughs. Rather we are talking about models constructed for the purpose of interactive visualization.

In order to frame the discussion, we begin with a description of non-automated urban construction. Some years ago we built a prototype 3D database of downtown Atlanta containing 471 buildings each with correct location, orientation, footprint, and height. The prototype was developed using graduate students contributing a large amount of manual labor. Image and terrain elevation data were selected and rectified to a State Plane coordinate system. Terrain ortho-correction of the images was unnecessary because of the low terrain relief in the Atlanta area; however, in many areas ortho-correction of imagery would be necessary. A road network of the city of Atlanta was obtained with street names and other transportation information and brought into the Arc/Info GIS (Fau93). Building footprints were obtained by manual photo interpretation and corroborated by field survey. Photo textures of major buildings within the downtown area were taken from perspective scene photographs of the Atlanta cityscape.

Individual buildings were identified and interactive techniques were used to extract their building textures and correct them to an orthogonal view. A team of students was dispatched from Georgia Tech to drive up and down each street in the Atlanta downtown. One student was the driver, two students took photographs on the left and the right as the car went down the street, one student noted building names and the street address of each building, and a fifth student checked the location on a printed map of the street network and tried to determine the type of business that was housed within the building.

There has been some research done on automated urban database construction. Prominent among these efforts is the MIT City Scanning Project (Bal99, Cho98, Coo99). This project uses machine vision to produce a useful representation of a scene, in particular to produce CAD models of structures in the scene. A pose-camera is mounted on a wheelchair-sized mobile platform with a GPS, heading information, and dead reckoning capability. The pose-camera acquires a spherical mosaic of images at selected positions along a path. These are then used to construct geometric models of objects in the environment. The goal is to produce a fully automated procedure for handling complex environments with thousands of structures. However, to date the system has only been used for several structures in the MIT square.

Instead of using static images, Zakhor and coworkers have extracted depth information from video sequences (Cha97, Sah99). In this work video collected along a limited set of paths is used to construct high fidelity 3D scenes that can then be navigated along many directions, even those not in the original set of paths. However these methods have only been applied indoors so far, and there are usually paths (e.g., under tables) that for which no video is available. Still the methods have useful byproducts for urban construction. For example, unwanted obstructions, such as trees or utility poles, can be automatically removed from the fronts of buildings to produce clean textures.

Laser-based methods, such as those using LIDAR, can produce extensive high-resolution height fields for urban areas. Usually extensive hands-on effort must be expended to separate buildings, trees, and other features from the terrain. Recently, however, some progress has been made in the automatic extraction of 3D models (Shi00).

4.   MODEL BUILDING STRATEGIES

Types of functions in an urban construction system can be separated into 1) Enhancement Techniques, 2) 2D Feature Extraction Techniques, 3) 3D

Object Extraction Techniques for Manmade Objects, and 4) 3D Object Extraction for Natural Features.

1.　Enhancement Techniques

Enhancement techniques are often needed to extract building information from imagery. Supplementary tools can be developed that utilize ephemeris and image header information to determine sun angle and azimuth. Area enhancement techniques can be used to brighten lower contrast image information within shadows. Low brightness regions within an image could then be identified and determined to be due to urban shadowing or other factors. Given this information and the scale of the image, shadows from buildings could be identified and used to determine building height. Because of the consistent sun angle within a small area, a small amount of ground truth information could be used to proportionally determine height of a number of buildings within an urban environment. Directional spatial filtering can be applied to enhance features and edges of shadow regions as well as transportation net features within the urban scene. Enhancement of shadow regions also will permit the use of urban images with cloud shadows.

2.　2D Feature Extraction Techniques

Multispectral pattern recognition is often used to determine land cover classification within color or multispectral images. This classification may be used as feature information to determine appropriate regions for urban extraction. This process could be optimized to operate sequentially on multiple resolution datasets to produce finer and finer approximations to the coverage of urban areas. Directed feature extraction could be applied in areas with high likelihood of urban features, and less processing would be required in other areas.

Most multispectral image classification techniques utilize traditional pattern recognition concepts to determine land cover information using spectral information as a color vector for each pixel within an image. Supervised and unsupervised classification techniques are applied on a pixel-by-pixel basis with no regard to the potential classification of neighboring areas. In many cases these classifications result in a salt and pepper speckled image that is often hard to interpret. Smoothing and post-processing filters are often applied to the classifications to reduce the noisy appearance.

We have done some preliminary work on the development of a multispectral image segmentation technique that considers spatial relationships between neighboring areas in the classification process. Edge enhancement, edge detection, and edge joining operations are performed in all spectral bands. The union of the multispectral-segmented images also has multispectral signatures attached to each segmented region. Unsupervised and/or supervised techniques may then be applied to identify the segmented regions. This approach is superior to traditional pixel-by-pixel pattern recognition (Nor96, Cam97, Sal92) in that the results are in polygon form, and size and shape factors can be used to identify building tops.

3.   Interactive 3D Object Extraction/Creation

The greatest single challenge in the creation of 3D urban landscapes is the efficient creation of accurate building representations. DFAD data may provide building footprints and height for major buildings in some areas. This should be used, if available, to supplement recent imagery of the candidate urban area. DFAD, like most GIS products, was created from imagery at some point, but may be out-of-date in the representation of the current urban environment. For example, destroyed buildings and new construction may not have been updated in the DFAD footprint file. High-resolution imagery, such as that provided commercially by Space Imaging and Earthwatch, could be used in conjunction with DFAD data, or in place of it, if it is not available. Digital imagery from these systems may be obtained with different look angles providing stereo. With appropriate camera models, photogrammetry techniques may be used to extract height of buildings using parallax. A simple interactive photogrammetric tool may be designed to extract relative height without a rigorous camera model. In the next section we describe some procedures to interactively apply close-range photogrammetry results to enhance building details.

In line with the needs of interactive visualization, the techniques described in the next section are not intended to produce detailed models of complex building shapes. They allow the creation of simpler rectangular shapes that may be phototextured for fast rendering. For buildings of complex shape, other techniques must be developed. One possibility is to use texture and geometry warping techniques that depend on the user's viewpoint. Thus 3D effects and lots of detail are retained while using much simpler geometry.

Once the rectangular block model is developed, one must define the image texture that would be associated with the sides of the block. One way to achieve this is to re-project the block building shape into the image space using photogrammetric parameters. A user can then fine-tune the building shape rectangular face to the actual texture associated with the selected building. At the click of a mouse button, the image texture is read from the image file and transformed into an orthogonal, rectangular texture. A more manual process is to draw a polygon containing the building texture, and this polygon is extracted and an orthogonal view created. We have implemented both techniques as described in the next section. Still to be done is the computation of levels of detail for both the textures and the building geometry. This is discussed in the section on real-time urban visualization below.

4. 3D Natural Object Extraction

In very high detail urban environments, trees and bushes must be considered as 3D objects. The prototype Georgia Tech campus model, for example, (Fau93, Dav99) has a representation for every tree within the campus as well as all of the buildings. Interactive location of trees using manual photo interpretation techniques is one approach to placing individual trees. An interactive tool that would make it easy to click on an individual tree and associate x, y, and z scale factors and an appropriate tree texture (scanned from traditional perspective color imagery) could be used to quickly populate a tree model placement file. A library of tree textures could then be created and made available as icons for interactive tree type selection.

A more automated approach to tree and bush placement might involve morphological image processing algorithms of erosion and dilation. (Har87, Mar87, Her88) In color aerial photographs, trees and their shadows are normally dark blobs compared to buildings, concrete, and grass areas within the image. Enhancement and simple classification techniques could be used to extract the image pixels likely to contain trees within the image. Dilation and erosion operators would then reduce each tree blob to a single point representing the position of the base of the tree. The width of the tree blob would provide information for scaling factor determination.

Complicating factors exist. Trees are often grouped in clumps with multiple trunks. An approach must be developed to address these groups in an interactive manner. In the urban environment trees are also likely to be found in the shadows of adjacent buildings. Separate enhancement of shadowed regions and subsequent tree processing must be developed.

5. SEMI-AUTOMATIC URBAN CONSTRUCTION

For fast, reliable production of urban terrains with large numbers of buildings, it is quite effective to equip a trained human interpreter with a flexible set of tools for creating detailed individual buildings, for bulk creation of buildings from an overhead image, and for visualization and final geographical placement of the created buildings. Here we describe an implementation of this approach (Was99).

With this approach the user first compiles one or more overhead photos of the urban area to be modeled. If close-up oblique images are available for selected buildings, one can use a close-range photogrammetry tool (for example, Eos Systems, Inc.'s PhotoModeler™) to create 3D models. Remaining buildings can be created from one or more overhead images. The user selects roof corners, base corners, and shadow extents, and a building with flat-topped textured roof is created of appropriate height (given the date and time a photo was taken). Building sides can be textured using texture images loaded into a texture library, or extracted from perspective-distorted images. In this approach the building models are exported into VGIS, a real-time 3D-landscape visualizer which places the urban terrain in its global setting. Here, final placement and adjustment of the buildings can be performed, and the user can explore and interact with the created urban terrain. We will discuss the use of VGIS further below in the section on real-time urban visualization.

The structure for the whole process of semi-automatic urban construction, database insertion, and visualization is illustrated in Figure 1. Overhead and oblique imagery in a variety of formats is transferred to a PC-based 3D Object Extraction system. In addition COTS close-range photogrammetry software extracts detailed 3D information from the oblique views. The 3D Object Extraction system creates building and other 3D feature models. These are collected and transferred using a modified Wavefront format to the VGIS Insertion Interface. After final positioning the building and feature models are inserted into the VGIS hierarchical structure. They are then available for real-time rendering.

1.   Overhead Imagery

Crucial to accurate scale and placement of buildings generated using these tools is the quality of the underlying overhead digital imagery. Images must be of sufficiently high resolution to allow the operator to swiftly and precisely select roof corner points. Also, to automatically generate the building heights, building shadows must be visible, and the precise time and date the imagery was collected must be known. Lastly, accurate geoplacement of the buildings will depend on the rectification of the overhead image.

To accurately place urban structures in their correct position on the Earth's surface, we must ultimately derive the correct lat/lon for given points in the overhead image. To this end, our software accepts imagery that has been geocorrected. Alternatively, there is limited geocorrection capability available in our software if raw overhead imagery is being used. If the user has 3 known reference points, a simple linear transformation can be performed. 2nd or 3rd order transformations are also available, if needed. It is important that one invests effort at this stage to obtain accurate georeferencing of urban structures, thus avoiding large-scale adjustments once the structures are put together in an urban database.

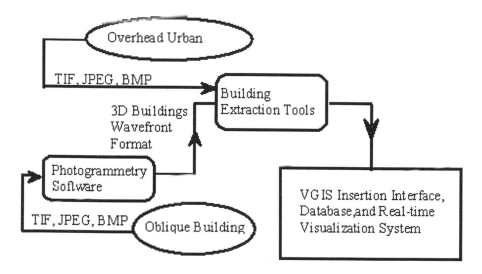

Figure 1. Schematic of the semi-automatic urban construction system

2. Time/Date Selection

It is useful if all urban images used with the urban construction tools have a known time and date of creation. Heights for structures that are in the center of the field of view cannot be derived from a single overhead image alone, and must be found from either time/date + shadow measurement, or from multiple oblique views using photogrammetry software. Height information can also be estimated if the number of stories (floors) is countable; this is a feature in the tools we provide.

3. Building Extraction

One is often faced with the problem of creating urban terrains with an uncertain quality and quantity of input imagery. To address this problem our approach is to remain as flexible as possible, enabling use of close-in oblique photos of structures if available, but not relying on these as a requirement.

Often, one does not have enough imagery to capture building texture and height from an overhead image. Or one may wish to capture from oblique views high resolution building textures not available in relatively low-resolution overhead images. It is also sometimes necessary to model "landmark" structures in detail, which is best accomplished by deriving 3D structure photogrammetrically from multiple oblique views. We wanted to use existing tools, only developing new tools where no equivalent existed. To that end, detailed building models are created using off-the-shelf photogrammetry software, while bulk building extraction from overhead photos is done using software we developed. Using a common platform, such as Windows NT, models from both tools can be quickly integrated.

There are a number of photogrammetry software products available for creation of 3D models from one or more photos. It is best to choose one that has several standard output formats (we use Wavefront format with extensions for collections of urban models). The software should also have the ability to use complex camera + lens models, or to use a default camera model with a single image, if one image is all that is available. Features (points, lines, and simple 3D primitives like cones and cylinders) are marked in one or more oblique images of the structure, and associated between images. In our system we can apply textures to the extracted structure from the image(s) the structure was created from, or we can use arbitrary texture images. We can then create a structure model and view it in a 3D-preview window. If it looks good, the system exports it in Wavefront format. VGIS imports this model, where final placement, rotation, and scaling operations can take place in a 3D world-view setting.

3.1   Building Polyhedra Generation

Rapid construction of urban terrains would be quite difficult and time-consuming if every building were modeled from multiple oblique views. Overhead imagery must be used to generate many of the buildings in the urban scene. Our approach is to give a human interpreter the ability to quickly select buildings, apply textures, create and save/export building models, and visualize created cities using Open GL under Windows NT.

For fast, semi-automated building extraction from an overhead photo, we developed software that employs simple user-selected flat-topped polyhedral building objects. It was found that automatic extraction of buildings using edge detection and other methods is prone to failure if the input image resolution and/or building-to-terrain contrast are not of sufficient quality. For rapid building creation, we employ a human interpreter for building corner/base-point/shadow selection. The user clicks on each corner of the building roof and adjusts the corners' 2D positions as needed. The user then anchors one roof corner to the building base (if the base is visible; i.e., if the building is not in the center of the image) by dragging an anchor line from a roof corner to the associated base corner. This is necessary for correct positioning of the building polyhedron on the surface plane. If a shadow is visible, the user drags a shadow line from a roof corner to it's associated shadow corner (Figure 2). At this point, the software has created a building model, correctly placed, with roof texture extracted from the overhead photo (Figure 3). If height has not been assigned (i.e., no shadow was specified, or no date/time was given for the overhead photo), the user may enter a height based on a priori knowledge of the height, estimation from the number of stories visible in the overhead image, or relative height to known buildings.

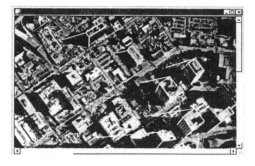

Figure 2. Roof Section, Anchoring and Shadow Selection

Figure 3. Untextured 3D Urban Terrain Preview Window

During the process of extraction, an identifier is placed with the model file describing the roof type of the individual buildings. As described above, flattop buildings have a top texture extracted from the image data. A library of standard roof types (e.g., peaked roofs or crest roofs) provides options for non-flat roofs. The user selects one and then attaches it at the appropriate scale and orientation by connecting corner points on the roof with corresponding points on the building top.

3.2   Building Textures

The sides of extracted buildings can be issued a single color value, but realism is significantly enhanced if actual building textures are applied. To this end, our extraction software supports texture extraction from oblique imagery (which can be overhead imagery, if the building in question is not in the center of the image and at least one side is visible). Images in BMP, JPEG, or TIFF format are loaded and selected for texture extraction. The desired texture corners are selected, regardless of perspective distortions in the image. The software then performs a projective mapping[3] (projection from one plane, through a point, onto another plane) of the selected arbitrary quadrilateral to a rectangular texture (Figure 4). This texture will have most of the perspective distortion removed, and will look like the building side as it would appear from an orthogonal view direction (with the exception of protrusive features). Extracted textures are added to a texture library. A thumbnail sheet is available for the user to select from, and apply, various textures to one or more buildings at a time (Figure 5). Any arbitrary texture can also be loaded into this library for use on buildings. Final adjustments to the buildings are made in the extraction window (Figure 6).

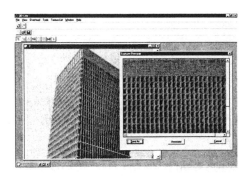

Figure 4. Texture Generation Using Projective Mapping

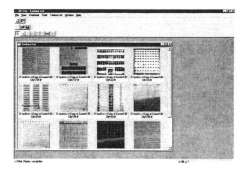

Figure 5. Texture Library Thumbnail Window

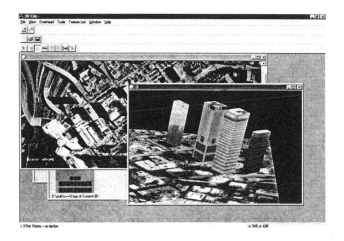

Figure 6. Textured Buildings in the Extraction Window

4. Exporting and Adjusting the Urban Terrain

Once the buildings in our urban terrain have been created, we export them using a modified Wavefront format which our visualization tool, VGIS, can import. The baseline ASCII Wavefront format was augmented with the following additions: geoplacement for each object (lat/lon coordinates), texture mapping, color selection, and full 3D rotation. VGIS uses these enhancements to correctly place building objects on the terrain. In addition this format permits transfer files containing multiple buildings (e.g., blocks) with correct relative placement.

It is necessary to interact visually with the created urban terrain to correct errors in placement and scale. This should occur in an environment with correctly placed terrain elevations and imagery. With such an integrated display one can quickly determine, for example, whether a line of buildings overlaps a street, is correctly positioned with respect to surrounding sets of buildings, or even if individual buildings correspond in position and scale to their footprints in an underlying phototexture. In addition interactive 3D visualization can expose height and scale inconsistencies between neighboring buildings. For this step (see Figure 1) we use VGIS because it is a powerful, immersive visualization tool for navigating virtual landscapes in real time and for viewing the urban landscape from any view or perspective. This is an ideal environment for our final urban terrain adjustment, because it allows us to place our city atop properly positioned elevation data & imagery, and to interact with (move, rotate, scale) new buildings with respect to existing ones. After final positioning of the buildings on the underlying terrain, the buildings are incorporated into the hierarchical VGIS object database, which enables real-time visualization through memory paging and level-of-detail. This process is described further below.

Figure 7. Oblique View of San Francisco Urban Database

5. Results for Building Urban Databases

To apply and evaluate our methods we built some urban databases for San Francisco and Savannah (Figures 7 and 8) and compared these with the previous, non-automated construction of the Atlanta database, described in Sec. 3. For a comparable number of buildings, the amount of effort for the semi-automated construction was 1/10th the man-hours of the non-automated construction. In addition to generic building geometry, we did some non-generic geometric construction for landmarks, such as the Transamerica building (Figure 9), using close-range photogrammetry. Only a few of the building shapes in the original Atlanta database were non-generic, and these were done by hand.

Figure 8. Oblique View of Savannah Urban Database

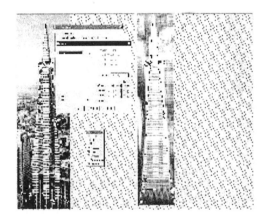

Figure 9. Close Range Photogrammetry of the Transamerica Building

6.   BACKGROUND WORK ON URBAN VISUALIZATION

Because of the potential and actual size of databases used in urban visualization, one must consider scalable techniques. Out-of-core techniques are necessary so that the system is not arbitrarily limited or greatly slowed by the amount of memory available. Previously our group has considered how out-of-core visualization applies to terrain and building datasets (Dav98, Dav99). We found that by combining out-of-core visualization, which tends to focus on 3D data, and visual simulation, which places an emphasis on visual perception and real-time display of multiresolution data, we obtain results for interactive terrain and building visualization with significantly improved data access and quality of presentation.

There has been other work that addresses interactive visualization of very large, out-of-core datasets. From what has been done so far, it is clear that application-control and domain-dependent data organization are essential to achieving good performance. Relying on system virtual memory, for example, frequently results in thrashing and abysmal performance. Ueng et. al. (Uen97) applies an application-controlled segmentation approach to out-of-core visualization. They spatially and hierarchically partition the dataset into an octree and load only needed segments. One problem with their approach is how to determine segment boundaries. Cox and Ellsworth present application-controlled demand paging (Cox97), in which the system knows something about what data are needed and when. By considering operating system memory management, they minimize thrashing. Zyda and co-workers (Fal93) came up with a hierarchical quadtree data structure by evenly subdividing data into square quadnodes and rendering with regular grid polygonalizations. Based on this regular grid they develop a paging method that takes into account the viewpoint and speed of the user. Recently Chiang et. al. (Chi98) has developed an interactive technique for out-of-core isosurface extraction from volume data. They developed a metacell technique for partitioning the original data and an indexing scheme for efficiently making isosurface queries into the metacells, which reside on disk, to bring in the appropriate data for constructing the isosurface. All the above out-of-core techniques consider the paging of continuous volumetric or terrain data. None considers application to collections of discrete 3D objects, as we do here.

The need to handle scalably large collections of buildings has come to the fore because, as described in the last section, there are improved methods to extract such data and because applications requiring accurate display of urban data (such as emergency response, urban planning, or urban warfare) are growing in importance.

7.   REAL-TIME URBAN VISUALIZATION

In this section we describe work we have done in real-time urban visualization. The techniques presented here have been inserted into VGIS. VGIS (Virtual Geographic Information System) is a real-time system for interactive display and navigation of global geospatial data (Lin97, Dav99, Fau00). In VGIS one can navigate continuously from outer space to a close-in view (with features at 1M resolution or smaller) and then fly close to the earth for hundreds of miles or more, if desired. VGIS treats the terrain as a single, connected surface for rendering using a "continuous, view-dependent" LOD representation (Lin96, Lin97, Fau00). Buildings, moving vehicles, multiple image layers including maps and phototextures, geographical annotations, and 4D weather phenomena can all be interactively displayed within VGIS. Thus the system must allow the navigation of and interaction with very large and high resolution, dynamically changing databases while retaining real-time display and interaction. A unique global hierarchical structure has been developed for this purpose. In this section the use of this hierarchical structure is described for buildings; a similar structure is used for terrain and other types of data within VGIS. VGIS also has interfaces to widely available government and commercial terrain and image databases and for Arc/Info, a major GIS query engine. The system allows users to navigate accurate geographies with sustained frame rates of 15-20 frames per second.

The VGIS data contain, among other things, terrain and extensive numbers of 3D objects (hundreds of buildings or more). The buildings are collected in groups but the groups may be distributed over a wide geographic area. Thus, as mentioned above, there are issues of out-of-core visualization since the data cannot be contained in memory but must be organized and brought in as needed from local or remote disks. Further a real-time system must manage detail of different types: for example, continuous height fields for terrain elevations, multiresolution imagery in various forms, and collections of 3D objects. All this heterogeneous detail must come together in a common visualization with fast enough display to maintain interactivity and permit effective navigation of the data.

There hasn't been much work done on urban detail management for interactive visualization. However, one promising approach uses the concept of "impostors" (Dec98). These are pre-generated, image-based representations that replace more distant collections of urban objects with multiple layers of textures meshes. The impostor captures relevant depth complexity in an urban model with textures and geometry that are much faster to draw than fully detailed representations. This approach has been used so far for urban walkthroughs where the viewer is at street level with much of the distant urban geometry occluded by nearby buildings. However, the approach shows promise for the more general problem of urban flythroughs where the user can be at any level below or above the urban skyline.

A powerful approach is to consider all data as part of a global geospatial collection. One can then locate and identify any piece of data in terms of lat/lon or related coordinates. Since even things in the atmosphere, such as weather, or under the ground tend to be contained in a thin band near the earth's surface (relative to the overall size of the earth), this should be an efficient way to organize geospatial volumetric data as well. Further it is likely that time-dependent or changing data may also be effectively included in this structure. This is a *GIS approach* to database structure and visualization, where the structure and visualization are considered as part of an integrated whole. This approach in line with new efforts in 3D urban GIS (Kon98) applied to urban planning, especially environmentally-oriented analyses, including noise, air pollution, urban climate, and so on. Kon98 provide an initial framework built around a hierarchical structure for 3D objects.

1. An Efficient Global Hierarchical Structure for Heterogeneous Data

A well-developed method from GIS (geographic information systems) is to use a quadtree hierarchical structure. However, when dealing with global data, a single quadtree can become cumbersome. We have developed a unique structure where the earth is divided into 32 zones, each 45° x 45° (Dav98, Lin97). (See Figure 10.) Each zone has its own quadtree; all are linked so that objects or terrain crossing quadrant boundaries can be rendered efficiently. We chose the number and extent of zones based on empirical observations of memory requirements, paging overhead, geometric accuracy, etc. A node in a quadtree corresponds to a raster tile of fixed dimensions and lat/lon resolution according to the level on which it appears in the quadtree. Quadnodes are identified by "quadcodes," which are built in a manner similar to the indices of representations of binary trees, that is, the children of a node with quadcode q are identified by $4q + 1$ through $4q + 4$. In addition, the quadcode contains a quadtree identifier that allows each quadcode to uniquely identify an area on the globe. This structure is replicated in the underlying disk management system so that files are aligned with the quadnodes in the set of linked quadtrees.

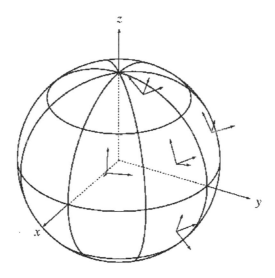

Figure 10. The Earth Divided into 32 Zones. The Labeled Axes Correspond to Earth Centered, Earth Fixed Cartesian XYZ Global Coordinate Systems for each Zone

The quadtrees also define the boundaries of local coordinate systems. If a single, geocentric coordinate system were used (with origin at the center of the earth), assuming 32-bit single precision floating point is used to describe object geometries, the highest attainable accuracy on the surface of the Earth is half a meter. Clearly, this is not sufficient to distinguish features with details as small as a few centimeters, e.g. the treads on a tank or detailed protrusive features on buildings. This lack in precision results in "wobbling" as the vertices of the geometry are snapped to discrete positions, which is present in other large scale terrain systems such as T_Vision (Gru95). We have developed an approach to overcome this problem (Lin97); we define a number of local coordinate systems over the globe, which have their origins displaced to the (oblate) spheroid surface that defines the Earth sea-level. The origins of the top-level coordinate systems are placed at the geographic centers (i.e. the mean of the boundary longitudes and latitudes) of the quadtree roots. While the centroid of the terrain surface within a given zone would result in a better choice of origin in terms of average precision, we decided for simplicity to opt for the geographic center, noting that the two are very close in most cases. The z axis of each coordinate system is defined as the outward normal of the surface at the origin, while the y axis is parallel to the intersection of the tangent plane at the origin and the plane described by the North and South poles and the origin. That is, the y-axis is orthogonal to the z-axis and locally points due North. The x-axis is simply the cross product of the y and z-axes, and the three axes form an orthonormal basis.

This choice of orientation is very natural as it allows us to approximate the "up" vector by the local z axis, which further lets us treat the terrain height field as a flat-projected surface with little error. Hence, the height field LOD algorithm, which is based on vertical error in the triangulation, does not have to be modified significantly to take the curvature of the Earth into account. However, the delta values (see (Lin96)) must be computed in Cartesian rather than geodetic coordinates to avoid over-simplification of constant-elevation but curved areas such as oceans. Figure 10 shows the local coordinate systems for a few zones.

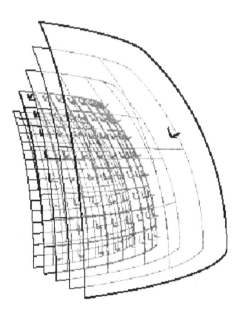

Figure 11. Nested Coordinate Systems in a Quadtree. 8 x 8 Smaller Coordinate Systems Appear 3 Levels Below the Root Node

Using the above scheme, the resulting worst case precision for a 45° x 45° zone is 25 cm---not significantly better than the geocentric case. We could optionally use a finer subdivision with a larger number of zones to obtain the required precision. However, this would result in a larger number of quadtrees, which is undesirable since the lowest resolution data that can be displayed is defined by the areal extent of the quadtree roots. Hence, too much data would be needed to display the lowest resolution version of the globe. Instead, we define additional coordinate systems within each quadtree. In the current implementation, we have added 256 x 256 coordinate systems within each quadtree---one coordinate system per node, eight levels below each root node---resulting in a 1 mm worst case precision. Figure 11 illustrates a subset of these nested coordinate systems. Terrain, object, and other managers keep track of which coordinate system to use among these thousands of systems and can even transition between coordinate systems for extended objects.

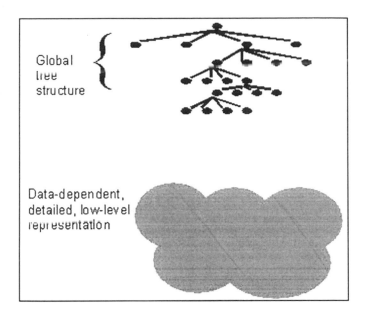

Figure 12. General Global Hierarchical Framework

The general approach to using the hierarchical structure is illustrated in Figure 12. In each zone the quadtree is traversed to a certain level, depending on the type of geospatial data. Below this level a non-quadtree detail management scheme is used that depends on the detailed characteristics of the data. Thus, for example, buildings and terrain have different levels at which separate non-quadtree detail management schemes take over. We describe the scheme for buildings further below.

This global hierarchical, nested structure will handle the earth and everything on it at levels of detail from global overviews to fine resolution close-ups. Navigation between these extremes involves changes of up to 10 or more orders of magnitude. We are now extending the structure to include everything over the earth, such as weather and other atmospheric effects (Fau00).

2.   Hierarchy for Buildings and Other Static Objects

At some level we must switch from the general geospatial quadtree to a non-quadtree detail management scheme that depends on the detailed characteristics of the data. What should this level be for buildings or other static objects? Let us assume a quadcell of side L_q. (The bounding box and bounding dimension in Figure 13 would be of order L_q.). Now let's assume an object with maximum dimension L_o. If $L_o < L_q$, then only the 8 surrounding quadcells might contain objects that would extend into a central quadcell. In fact if we divide the central cell into 4 quadrants and further assume that all objects are placed in the quadcells that contain their centers, the maximum number of quadcells whose objects could overlap this quadrant would be 4, the central cell plus the 3 nearest quadcells to the quadrant. Our approach is to go as deeply as possible using the very efficient quadtree but not to permit more than 4 neighboring (or "linked") cells for considering overlapping objects, since there will be increased overhead from keeping track of the links and from having to consider all the objects in the linked cells. The collection of objects in the linked cells would have to be considered in view frustum culling, collision detection, and many other operations. Thus we choose cells for which $L_o < L_q$. For buildings in an urban setting, L_o could be about 50 meters, the dimension of a typical city block. If a typical building is the size of a house, say 10 meters on a side, we would have to consider on average no more than 100 or so buildings for 4 linked cells. Note that occasionally we will have to consider linked cells that could be in more than one quadtree, but this can be handled with appropriate pointers.

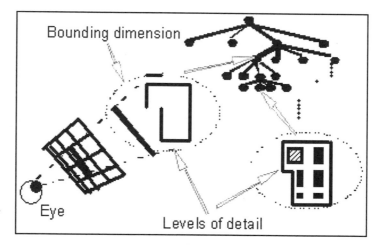

Figure 13. Detailed Low-Level Representation for Buildings with Screen-Based Threshold
Using Bounding Dimension

The hierarchy permits a simple but effective detail management process. Object pointers are loaded at the quadlevel determined as described above. Accompanying the pointer is the object location and a bounding dimension obtained from the largest dimension of the object bounding box. Using the viewpoint, object location, and bounding dimension, the system finds a maximum size for the object in screen space in terms of pixels. (See Figure 13.)

However, what about extended objects such as a stadium, the Pentagon, the Vehicle Assembly Building at the Kennedy Space Center, or very large objects created via detail management? The latter might require considering several blocks as one object. If we use the largest such object in the database to determine the leaf node level of the quadtree, we might also end up with cells containing several hundred smaller objects. To obviate this problem we have discrete representations of such large objects at successive levels of the quadtree, each representation carrying its own list of linked cells. Thus if we flew from outer space down towards an urban area, we might first see a phototextured shape representing the downtown area, which would then be replaced by more detailed shapes representing collections of blocks and tall landmark buildings, and finally these would be replaced by shapes for individual buildings. Although the present system switches between discrete representations, one can imagine a more sophisticated process with more continuous switching of detail.

Since such large objects are relatively small in number, we can handle them reasonably efficiently even though they carry their own lists and descriptions. Also such representations usually occur before the appearance of large numbers of smaller objects. When considering small buildings at urban densities, however, we use our more automated and compact linked cell mechanism.

3. Hierarchical Structure for Optimized Paging

As discussed above our global structure is divided into 32 zones, each 45^0 x 45^0. Each quadrant has its own quadtree; all are linked so that objects or terrain crossing quadrant boundaries can be rendered correctly. To improve performance, the VGIS system is divided into multiple threads that can run in parallel. In particular, there is an independent rendering thread, which has a "triple buffer" of display lists (Lin97). One of the display lists contains what the renderer is currently drawing, one is used by the scene manager to buffer graphics commands, and the last contains data that are ready to be displayed.

Each paging thread, such as those for objects and terrain, has a server and manager. The object server loads pages from disk while the manager decides which cells should be loaded (taking into account user viewpoint and navigational speed) and passes it along to the scene manager. The object server and manager communicate with the scene manager and the rest of the system via shared caches, so that communication is limited to small request messages and acknowledgments. This communication path supports a demand-paging approach such as that of Cox and Ellsworth (Cox97). When data are needed for a node in the quadtree, the scene manager allocates space in the shared cache and sends a message via a shared memory priority queue to the object manager. Message priorities in this queue are changed dynamically according to the importance of the associated request as determined by the scene manager. Thus, requests that gradually become less important sift towards the end of the queue and get serviced only when no higher priority requests remain in the queue.

The underlying disk management system has a file structure with files aligned with the quadnodes in the set of linked quadtrees. Put together, all this makes the geospatial visualization system quite scalable. Tens to hundreds of gigabytes of data can be made available for visualization, either locally or remotely.

Object Page Scheduling. We have found that the above page priority procedure sometimes falls short when handling global data. Users of such data frequently fly quickly from a global view where the terrain elevation and imagery data are at 8 Km resolution to views close to the ground where the data are at 1 M resolution or higher, and there may be hundreds or more buildings in view. If the user flies in too fast, the traversal of linked quadtrees by the manager falls well behind the user's navigation. The process can stall in this case, and the pages for the scene currently in view can take quite long to arrive.

Unfortunately the system cannot just jump to the appropriate position in the quadtree. The quadtree has to be traversed to get important properties information, especially quadcell linking data but also geospatial bounding boxes and other data, that are necessary to determine if the object data should be displayed or not. To address this problem we created a modified version (Dav99) of the separate set of indexing trees used in the quadtree paging system. This separate structure provides properties information but is lightweight so it can be traversed quickly. Large segments of the indexing trees reside in main memory for fast access. With the flexibility of this scheme we can skip one or more levels before paging in object data. A predictive mechanism is instituted based on user navigational speed and viewing direction to help predict where the terrain manager should skip.

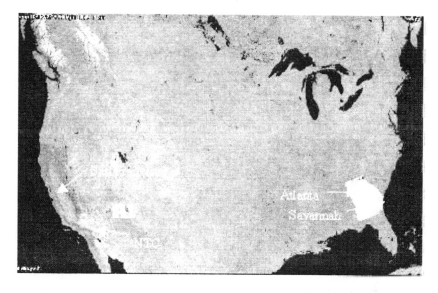

Figure 14. Overview Showing Locations of Building Datasets in the VGIS Hierarchical Structure

Since the scene manager is receiving continuous updates from the user via the user interface, it can use these in its requests to the object manager. The scene manager can, for example, expend more detail on buildings or other objects in the center of the screen, since this is where the user's attention is likely to be focused.

4. Results for Collections of Buildings

We have tested our methods by inserting several sets of buildings at different geographic locations, which are identified on the U.S. overview in Figure 14. From the overview we can fly continuously into any of these urban areas, as shown in Figures 15-16. For each area there may be not only buildings but also high resolution terrain. Atlanta, for example, (Figure 15) has terrain elevations and phototextured imagery at 1-M resolution, embedded in a surrounding area at 10-M resolutions, which is nested in the state of Georgia at 100-M resolution. With hierarchical paging of buildings, one can fly around unimpeded until one gets close to a particular urban area, at which time only the buildings in view are paged in.

Figure 15. Fly-In to Close-Up View of Atlanta Buildings

Figure 16. Fly-In to Buildings at the National Training Center (NTC)

To illustrate the capability of our method, we recorded in Table 1 results for flying continuously from the overview in Figure 14 to the close-up view of Atlanta in Figure 15. In this case the global database contained 2 collections of nearly 500 buildings each, one in Atlanta and one at the National Training Center (NTC). We have gotten similar results with databases that include the rest of the building sets identified in Figure 16. We used an SGI Infinite Reality with 4 R10000 processors, 1 GB of memory, and 27 GB of disk. All results were obtained on continuous fly-in with no pauses.

Table 1. Comparison of Frame Rates without Buildings, with Buildings (without Hierarchical paging), and with Buildings (with Hierarchical Paging)

	13.6×10^6 M	672×10^3 M	235×10^3 M	1.92×10^3 M	810 M
Without buildings	59 frames per second (fps)	30 frames per second	30 frames per second	28 frames per second	28 frames per second
With buildings no paging	15 fps 485 buildings	12 fps 485 buildings	11 fps 485 buildings	6 fps 485 buildings	5 fps 485 buildings
With buildings with paging	59 fps 0 buildings	30 fps 23 buildings	19 fps 126 buildings	10 fps 485 buildings	20 fps 485 buildings

In Table 1 distance in meters is tabulated horizontally and type of method is listed vertically. For all methods frame rate goes down as one flies closer to the high resolution terrain in Atlanta. Table 1 shows that the method with buildings but without hierarchical paging has a rather low frame rate throughout, even in the global overview. The method with buildings and paging starts with a frame rate the same as that for no buildings and decreases only as the viewer moves closer to the city. Note that as one flies close to Atlanta (at 1.92×10^3 M and 810 M) the frame rate goes up for the method with hierarchical paging compared to that without hierarchical paging, even though all buildings are paged in at that point. The reason is the more efficient culling that goes on with the paging method. Also note that buildings are paged in even when the viewer is rather far away. This is because of the conservative 1-pixel threshold chosen for the paging and also because of lack of levels of detail. For example, if we chose an intermediate object pasted with a phototexture of the buildings and with only a few of the most prominent buildings in 3D, the frame rate would be significantly higher at middle distances. We have tested this and found significantly improved frame rate with little degradation of visual appearance. For all tests a fly-in from outer space typically took 30 seconds or less. During that process there was no noticeable delay in paging and display of buildings.

Buildings in groups of any size can be placed all over the earth and neither performance *nor* memory load is affected till the user is relatively close to the buildings. Additionally, the effective handling of culling makes feasible the handling of extended building collections that are much larger than the ones considered here. In fact, we are planning to test such an extended collection by replicating the current sets of buildings several times side-by-side.

8.   CONCLUSIONS

We have developed a Windows NT-based toolset for rapid creation of urban structures from overhead and oblique photos, and for visualization of these created structures. We have shown that a human operator can effectively create a rich 3D urban terrain using a small suite of software tools. This provides the flexibility to handle multiple types of input imagery, and to scale the time invested in creating a building with its relative importance in the scene. In applying these tools to the development of several urban databases, we have shown that development effort is reduced by an order of magnitude or more over previous non-automated methods. Further databases can be built from the rich variety of sources now available. We have even done photogrammetry and extracted textures from building images available on the Web. In the future faster and more accurate methods may be obtained by combining the semi-automated methods described here with automated methods for extracting models from imagery or streaming video.

We have presented results for real-time visualization of out-of-core collections of 3D objects. This is a significant extension of previous methods and shows the generality of hierarchical paging procedures applied to global geospatial environments. For buildings, the results show the effectiveness of using a screen-based paging and display criterion within a hierarchical framework. The screen-based tolerance is adjustable and directly provides a control for image quality.

The results demonstrate that our method is scalable since it is able to handle multiple collections of buildings (e.g., cities) placed around the earth with full interactivity and without extensive memory load. Further the method shows efficient handling of culling and is applicable to larger, extended collections of buildings. Finally, the method shows that levels of detail can be incorporated to provide improved detail management.

We plan to extend this geospatial hierarchical framework to other types of objects and data. For example we are working on large collections of moving or real-time updateable objects. These might be vehicles on the terrain or results from receivers or sensors that are inserted in real-time. We are also working on the organization and display of dynamic, 3D fields such as weather in the same framework.

9.   FUTURE DIRECTIONS

Ongoing improvements include the addition of a roof template library (for application of various roof types to our buildings), a more intuitive user interface for building extraction, enhancements to the level-of-detail algorithms in VGIS (how to represent cities and individual buildings at arbitrary view angles and distances). The advent of new and higher resolution types of image data will allow further automation of the urban reconstruction process. Automated tools for extracting elevation data from stereo photography or detailed elevation creation tools such as LIDAR could provide geocorrected elevation height fields that would show the height of buildings. The rendering of these detailed elevation data sets with draped phototexture is unsatisfactory for two reasons: 1) the phototexture from the source image is simply smeared over the building sides and edges of buildings are occasionally rounded due to insufficient resolution and 2) the rendering speed for these detailed height fields will plummet due to the unnecessary large number of terrain polygons. A methodology could be developed that uses the extracted, geocorrected height fields to identify sharp height offsets and associate the height of the terrain elevation feature with a 3 D object associated with that location. This information could be directly fed back into the height of object variable and compared to the height associated with shadow length and other tools such as close range photogrammetry. The resulting tool would have the effect of "cutting down" the trees and buildings and replacing them with 3 D objects, leaving a "bald earth" Digital Terrain Model (DTM) for real-time rendering. The use of oblique imagery within our existing tool would allow correct association of building textures to the 3-D objects.

10. ACKNOWLEDGEMENTS

We acknowledge the work of Tony Wasilewski and Frank Jiang on development of software and evaluation of results. This work is supported by two grants from the National Science Foundation and by funding from the Office of Naval Research and the Naval Research Lab.

Bala, K., Dorsey, J., and Teller, S (1999). Interactive Ray-Traced Scene Editing Using Ray Segment Trees. Proceedings of Tenth Eurographics Workshop on Rendering, Granada, Spain, pp. 31-44.

Campbell N.W., Thomas, B.T., and Troscianko, T. (1997). A Two-Stage Process for Accurate Image Segmentation. Sixth International Conf. On Image Processing and Its Applications, IEE.

Chang, NL and A. Zakhor, A. (1997). View generation for three-dimensional scenes from video sequences. IEEE Transactions on Image Processing, Vol.6, no.4, pp. 584-598.

Chiang Y., Silva, C., and Schroeder, W.J. (1998). Interactive Out-of-Core Isosurface Extraction. *IEEE Visualization '98*, pp. 167-174.

Chou, G.T. and, Teller, S. (1998). Multi-Level 3D Reconstruction with Visibility Constraints. Proceedings of Image Understanding Workshop.

Coorg, S. and Teller, S. (1999). Extracting Textured Vertical Facades from Controlled Close-Range Imagery. Proceedings of CVPR, pp. 625-632.

Cox, M., and Ellsworth, D. (1997). Application-Controlled Demand Paging for Out-of-Core Visualization. Proceedings, *IEEE Visualization '97*, pp. 235-244.

Davis, D., Jiang, T.Y., Ribarsky, W., and Faust, N. (1998). Intent, Perception, and Out-of-Core Visualization Applied to Terrain. Report GIT-GVU-98-12, pp. 455-458, *IEEE Visualization '98.*

Davis, D., Ribarsky, W., Jiang, T.Y., Faust, N., and Ho, S. (1999). Real-Time Visualization of Scalably Large Collections of Heterogeneous Objects. Report GIT-GVU-99-14, pp. 437-440, IEEE Visualization '99.

Decoret, X., Schaufler, G., Sillion, F., and Dorsey, J. (1998). Multi-layered impostors for accelerated rendering. Computer Graphics Forum, Vol.18, 3, pp. C61-72.

Falby, J.S., Zyda, M.J., Pratt, D.R., and Mackey, R.L. (1993). NPSNET: Hierarchical Data Structures for Real-Time Three-Dimensional Visual Simulation. *Computers & Graphics* 17(1), pp. 65-69.

Faust, N. (1993). Virtual GIS, A New Reality. Proc. of Third International Conference on Urban Planning and Urban Management -Atlanta.

Faust, N., Ribarsky, W., Jiang, T.Y., and Wasilewski, T. (2000). Real-Time Global Data Model for the Digital Earth. Proceedings of the International Conference On Discrete Global Grids .

Grueneis, G. P., Mayer, J., and Schmidt, A. (1995). T_Vision. *Visual Proc. of SIGGRAPH 95*, p. 134.

Haralick R.M., Sternberg, S.R., and Zhuang, X. (1987). IEEE Trans. PAMI, Vol. PAMI-9, No.4 pp. 532-550.

Hertz, L. and Schafer, R. (1988). Multilevel Thresholding Using Edge Matching. Computer Vision, Graphics, and Image Processing, Vol.44, pp. 279-295.

Koninger, A., and S. Bartel., S. (1998). 3D-GIS for Urban Purposes. GeoInformatica, Vol.2, No. 1 pp. 79-103.

Lindstrom, P., Koller, D., Ribarsky, W., Hodges, L., Faust, N., and Turner, G. (1996). Real-Time Continuous Level of Detail Rendering of Height Fields. Report GIT-GVU-96-02, SIGGRAPH '96, pp. 109-118.

Lindstrom P., Koller, D., Ribarsky, W., Hodges, L., and Faust, N. (1997). An Integrated Global GIS and Visual Simulation System. Report GIT-GVU-97-07.

Maragos P. and Schafer, R. (1987). Morphological Filters: Parts I and II. IEEE Transactions on Acoustics, Speech, and Signal Processing, Vol. ASSP-35, No.8, pp. 1153-1184.

Noriega, L. (1996). A Feature-Based Approach to Color Image Segmentation. Transactions of the Third International Conference on the Applications of Computer Systems, Szczecin, Poland.

Shinya, M., Miyagawa, S., Horiguchi, K., and Uemoto, N. (2000). Automatic construction of three-dimensional virtual urban models: towards three-dimensional maps. NTT R & D, Vol.49, no.1, pp.11-18.

Sahouria, E., and Zakhor, A. (1999). Content Analysis of Video Using Principal Components. IEEE Transactions on Circuits and Systems for Video Technology, Vol.9, no.8, pp.1290-1298.

Salembier, P., and Serra, J. (1992). Morphological Multiscale Segmentation of Images. Proc. of SPIE Visual Communication and Image Processing 92, Vol.1818, p. 620 –Boston.

Ueng, S.K., Sikorski, C., and Ma, K.L. (1997). Out-of-Core Streamline Visualization on Large Unstructured Meshes. *Transactions on Visualization and Computer Graphics* 3(4), pp. 370-379.

Wasilewski, T., Faust, N., and Ribarsky, W. (1999). Semi-Automated and Interactive Construction of 3D Urban Terrains. Vol. 3694A, *Proceedings of the SPIE Aerospace/Defense Sensing, Simulation & Controls Symposium*, pp. 31-38.

Index